A CIVIL WAR REENACTOR'S GUIDEBOOK

TIPS AND SUGGESTIONS FROM THE FIELD

GREG M. ROMANECK

HERITAGE BOOKS
2007

IHERITAGE BOOKS
AN IMPRINT OF HERITAGE BOOKS, INC.

Books, CDs, and more—Worldwide

For our listing of thousands of titles see our website at
www.HeritageBooks.com

Published 2007 by
HERITAGE BOOKS, INC.
Publishing Division
65 East Main Street
Westminster, Maryland 21157-5026

Copyright © 2007 Greg M. Romaneck

Cover design by Kyle M. Romaneck

All rights reserved. No part of this book may be reproduced or transmitted in any form or by any means, electronic or mechanical, including photocopying, recording or by any information storage and retrieval system without written permission from the author, except for the inclusion of brief quotations in a review.

International Standard Book Number: 978-0-7884-4363-1

INTRODUCTION

Living historians are often people who strive to develop a deeper understanding of the Civil War era. Some people focus in upon the finer details of uniforms, equipment, and other elements of the material reality of that epoch. Other individuals strive to grasp the tactics, drill, and military procedures of the age. For some it is the social history of the common soldier's experience that grabs their interest. Whatever the focus, people engaged in living history, or who have an interest in the Civil War time period in general, benefit from a more well grounded understanding of the stories the wartime survivors left behind them.

There are hundreds of memoirs and other primary source accounts crafted by Civil War veterans available to read if you wish to. Reading such material enhances the ability of a student or reenactor to more fully comprehend the experiences of those men and women who fought the Civil War. Additionally, for those people who do don uniforms or period authentic attire there is always room to improve our experience of living history.

What follows is a book encompassing twenty-three chapters aimed at enhancing your ability to make Civil War reenacting a meaningful and worthwhile hobby. The selections focus in on a wide range of subjects inclusive of practical suggestions related to camping, marching, gear, attitudes, and reflection. There are also chapters dedicated to practical tips to living historians in more philosophical areas such as morale, burn out, and reenacting in difficult times. Some chapters offer primary source information relative to language, wellness, and period beliefs. All of the entries are designed to help reenactors, and their comrades, have a more enjoyable time of it in the field.

The Civil War is an age that has fascinated this writer since he was a wee lad. For over twelve years I have also pursued the sometimes - improbable hobby of Civil War reenacting. It is hoped that some of the words contained within this volume will be of at least minimal interest to you. Take care and try to remember both the sacrifices of our 19th century predecessors and the enjoyment that is inherent in this hobby.

GMR

Dedication: This book is dedicated to all those men, women, and children who don period clothes and head out to the reenacting fields in all sorts of conditions to help keep the memory of the Civil War alive.

Table of Contents

1.	Civil War School Presentations	1
2.	The Unfinished Civil War	11
3.	Servant Leadership	19
4.	Racism & Reenacting	27
5.	Strategies to Avoid Reenactor "Burnout"	35
6.	Maintaining Good Foot-Care in the Field	43
7.	Artillery Safety: A Case Study	53
8.	Leadership & the Artillery Gun Sergeant	65
9.	Roles & Responsibilities in Civil War Artillery	77
10.	Reenacting in Wartime	87

11.	Sleeping Without a Tent	96
12.	Ten Reasons to be an Artilleryman	106
13.	Commonly Used Civil War Language	112
14.	Living History in a Time of Crisis	120
15.	Reenactor Leave of Absence	130
16.	Taking a Hit	140
17.	Civil War Illnesses	148
18.	Civil War Remedies	156
19.	Fielding Questions	162
20.	Reenactor's Bookshelf: Artillery	172
21.	Women Warriors	186
22.	Top Picks for Younger Readers	194

| 22. | Top Picks fro Younger Readers | 193 |

| 23. | "Dear Emma" : | |
| | Letters to & from the Homefront | 211 |

| 24. | Tips for Women Soldiers | 223 |

| 25. | Civil War Combat Attitudes: | |
| | Maintaining A Soldierly Bearing | 239 |

Two Poems   249

- Chapter 1 -

Civil War School Presentations: SUGGESTIONS AND TIPS TO HELP YOU AND THE STUDENTS GET THE MOST OUT OF THEM

Sooner or later, most reenactors are called upon to come to a classroom to share their knowledge about the Civil War. From my own experiences as teacher, school administrator, and frequent schoolroom presenter, I have learned that some forethought on the part of reenactors can make school presentations one of the most satisfying experiences we can engage in. Sharing what we know about the lives of our ancestors is a true act if living history. If we want to do this in a way that will stir an interest in learning more about our history, we need to engage students in a manner in which is most likely to capture their interest. So here are some thoughts about going through the schoolhouse door in your wools.

Know Your Audience

Having presented to students from kindergarten through college, I have found that there are different needs, interests, and abilities at each point along the age continuum. Each age group presents unique opportunities and challenges to the presenter. Therefore,
it is important to know ahead of time what age group you are presenting to.

Students in primary grades will respond to hands-on approaches much better than high school students. Middle school students are more likely to look for the "blood and guts" of history. High school students will probably be better able to enter into a discussion about you presentation.

Tailor the artifacts, materials, stories and book recommendations to the group you will be working with. For example, when working with third or fourth graders, it is appropriate to pass around your canteen, belt, and other pieces of gear. Younger students learn better when they can see and touch. On the other hand, it is probably not a good idea to ask a junior high level American History class for volunteers to come up front and dress as a Confederate. High school students can act bored or detached. When working with older students, it may be best to gather questions in advance from the students and teacher, and work from these. Here are a few general guidelines for different age groups:

Elementary School – Use a hands on approach, passing materials around; allow for many student questions; do not talk or lecture for long periods on any one topic; watch your vocabulary, and give lots of positive feedback to the audience such as, "that was a good question".

Middle School – Allow for demonstrations with the student participation; use a hands-on approach; ask the group questions; check to see what the group is interested in; be prepared for more disruptive behavior and try to limit the size of the group.

High School – Address subjects the students are interested in, and use open-ended questions, such as "was slavery the cause of the war?"; get more in depth with the topic; involve the teacher in the dialog; connect the issues of the 19th century with the present.

Beyond the age level of the class, try to find other elements of the class makeup. An honors group working with enriched material should have more questions and a deeper understanding of the period than might normally be the case. Conversely, a group with learning or behavioral challenges may not understand the language or concepts you typically include in your presentation. When you are presenting to a more academically challenged group, be more interactive and use words that are concrete rather than abstract. All children can learn. By knowing your audience, you can help them to do so.

Audience Size Counts

I have had the opportunity to present to special education classes as small as six children and to middle and elementary groups as large as 450 students. The size of your group will affect what you do and how you do it. The larger the group you are speaking to, the more diverse the behavior will be. As you increase your number of students, the less personal interaction there will be between you and any given student. Also, your own comfort level may well change due to the number of people in the audience.

Larger groups require more planning and some changes of pace. If you rely heavily on questions from the students to fill out your time, know that it is unlikely that as many students will volunteer in a group of one hundred as in one of thirty. So, if you are going to work with a group that is very large, you should plan on doing more demonstrations and less discussion. You might ask for a volunteer or two to join you and dress in the various uniforms.

Children in elementary and middle school grades have moderately short attention spans. To engage them in what you have to offer build in a number of transitions into your presentation. In large groups, involve the teaching staff. If the students do not have many questions, turn to the teachers and ask for suggestions about people and events the class would like to know more about. Another strategy is to ask the class for a list of questions before you arrival. This way, you can address their interests, even if individual students are hesitant to ask questions during the presentation.

It is also possible that, in a large group, you will be working with a range of age levels. I remember a presentation I made, along with civilian reenactor and a friend dressed as a Confederate, to an entire grade school. When confronted with children as young as five and as old as eleven, our trio of presenters had to work very hard translating our comments so that everyone in the audience could get something out of our efforts.

In working with smaller groups, from 20 to 60 students, the challenges are far different. You can personalize the information much more. Passing around items of clothing, artifacts, or other Civil War materials becomes an option. Students can sit much closer to the presenter, and smaller groups allow for a freer flow of questions and answers.

In a group of twenty-five fourth graders, it is possible for each child to handle the hardtack or come up at the end of the presentation to see everything you are wearing. When preparing for a smaller group, it still is a good idea to ask the teacher to work with the students to generate a list of questions. By having the class think about your presentation ahead of time, it is easier to make it an extension of the curriculum. Remember--good teaching requires preparation and organization.

You Are Not The Dean

Inevitably, any reenactor who does frequent presentations will encounter some groups who are less interested in what he has to say. In some cases, behavior problems can occur during a presentation. Remember, you are a guest and not the dean of students. Rely upon the teacher for discipline.

It might be appropriate to remind a class that " I really can better answer your questions if you raise your hand" or "I'm having some trouble hearing John's question because others are talking". However, it is the teacher's job to make sure that the atmosphere in the classroom is one conducive to learning. If you reach the point where you are distracted by what the students are doing, or you feel you are not being heard, it is fair to say to the teacher, "I think we need to get our group refocused" or "Ms. Smith, do you think we are having trouble listening as a group?"

Usually, the simple novelty of your dress and appearance should result in at least a reasonably well behaved group. But if things are not going well, draw upon the teachers to restore order.

Watch Your Mouth

In presentations, the words you choose are what you will live and die by. I have seen some wonderful reenactors trying to describe things to younger children with words that none of the students understood. It is vital to match what you are saying to the audience.

When working with elementary students, be as concrete as possible in your language. When speaking of slavery, explain that it means being able to own another person. Do not use words such as servitude, indenture, peonage, or bondage. The children probably will not know what you are talking about.

Always be careful to let the group know that we, as living historians, are not glorifying war. From 1861 to 1865, more than 600,000 Americans died as a result of the Civil War. To paraphrase Uncle Billy Sherman, "war is all hell, and you cannot refine it". A reenactor who fails to point out the horrors of war and its entire attendant suffering has failed in a basic way. Be careful that the way in which you communicate what you know about the 19th century does not appear to be a justification for violence and destruction in the 20th century. Avoid technically complicated explanations of weapons. Most reenactors include some form of musket demonstration in their presentations. In addition to the obvious stricture against bringing ammunition to a school, shy away as well from the specifics of muzzle velocity, caliber, or the specifications of weapons. The students will be very interested in what the musket looks like, how it was loaded, what a Minie ball is, the kinds of wounds it could inflict, and other details of how it worked. It is very unlikely that many students will be terribly interested in all the technical mechanics of each gun. Temper your own interests in weapons with the knowledge that students may not share it.

Finally, never use profanity on school grounds. I know from personal experience when participating in a 'Civil War day' at a middle school that people can forget this rule. This can result in embarrassment to the teachers, principal, and reenactors. Be sure to present yourself as a role model to the children and mind your language.

Humor Is OK

School can be a wonderful place for children, but it can also be dry as dust. Sadly, many people see history as a seemingly endless stream of dates, names, and dead people. As living historians we have an opportunity to put life back into our field of study.

Come prepared to share not only factual information about great men, battles and campaigns, but to tell children what life was like during the Civil War. If you spend a great deal of time talking about dates, battles, and leaders, you become nothing more than a form of animated textbook. I have found that very little of my time in presentations is spent talking about either generals or battles. Most of what I do is discuss the day-to-day life of common men and women. This approach will have the greatest chance of capturing the interest of students.

Living historians can offer much more than what is contained in the homogenized texts that the students have to read. Bring stories and tales into your presentation. If you can, tell stories that let students see how soldiers kept their morale and sense of humor. Stories about recreational activities such as louse races, baseball, and practical jokes are generally well received by students. Bringing humor into the classroom is a good way of catching their interest. By touching upon both the humorous and the tragic, we paint an accurate picture of the age.

In general, talk about incidents that affected individuals. Students want to know what happened to individual people and families. Recite portions of letters. Share stories of your own family from the period, if you have them. By sharing the human element of the Civil War, we can help stimulate an understanding of the people whose era we love so much.

Know Your Stuff

It is a truism, which I personally disagree with, that "those who can, do--those who cannot, teach". In my own experience, I see no nobler field than teaching. When you enter a school as a presenter you don the mantle of a teacher, so be sure you have something to offer. Be prepared in the same way that a classroom teacher needs to be prepared.

Reenactors who often do school presentations have a general outline of what they plan to cover. Key themes such as medical care, daily routines, weaponry, emancipation, the role of women, Illinois in the Civil War, etc., are commonly part of each presentation that I do. But I am constantly reading and learning about the Civil War era, and each year try to have some new information to share. By changing some of the content, I help keep my presentations alive, not only for the students, but for myself.

Read whatever you can about our era. Simply wearing a uniform and shouldering a musket does not prepare you to be a good presenter. You have to know a great deal about life in the 1860s to educate our children about the Civil War. I have found that most of my Civil War reading in the past few years has focused on social history or primary source books. Reading works about what it felt like to march in the mud, how camps were set up, and how the wounded or dead were treated has deepened my own feeling for the period. If you do not do a great deal of reading about the Civil War, it will be more difficult for you to have the information needed to provide more than a superficial approach to the war.

Presentations to students should not be the domain of individuals who simply like to dress up. While a doctorate in history is not required to talk about the Civil War, it certainly is important to have enough information to do justice to the needs of the students whose lives you touch.

Beyond your own reading and preparation, be able to recommend books to the teacher and pupils. Staff appreciates it when you are able to identify books about the Civil War that might be available at the school. Develop your own list of books appropriate for different ages. Do not expect a middle school student to know that Jim Murphy's *Boy's War* or Ina Chang's *A Separate Battle: Women and the Civil War* would be books worth reading. Also, do not expect every elementary teacher to be familiar books such as Patricia Polacco's *Pink and Say*. Come prepared with a list of recommended reading and share it.

Reenactors can do a great service for children and enjoy themselves at the same time by doing school presentations. By keeping in mind the needs of the audience and preparing for your presentation, you can help children learn something of their country's past and possibly stir their interest in the rest of our nation's history. In a very real sense, by helping children to learn about the events and people of the Civil War we do a service both to our generation and the one that lived through those momentous events.

– Chapter 2 –

The Unfinished Civil War: A Reenactor's PR Nightmare

On Monday, February 19, 2001, The History Channel aired the latest Greystone Communications Civil War documentary. In this instance the film, entitled *The Unfinished Civil War,* was focused on the topic of reenacting and those diehards who strive to recreate Civil War history in an authentic manner. This film marked one of the first times that a nationally aired TV special was centered upon "The Hobby" and presented a unique opportunity for the viewing public to get a first hand look at reenactors and their heartfelt commitment to living history. Sadly, after watching *The Unfinished Civil War* this writer was left with nothing but shame regarding our hobby.

While The Unfinished Civil War is a well produced and carefully filmed production the net effect it will have upon viewers is unfortunate. The film itself features interviews with reenactors as well as a juxtaposition of the Confederate battle flag controversy that erupted in 1999. Through shots of reenactors preparing for, participating in, and reacting to events the viewers are introduced to some of the common features of Civil War reenacting. Events such as Gettysburg, Olustee, Cedar Creek, and South Mountain are each featured with interviews of living historians and action footage. In addition, a significant amount of time in this 90-minute film is dedicated to interviews with various parties relative to the appropriateness of the Confederate flag being displayed on the South Carolina capitol building in

Columbia. While these topics combine in an interesting fashion the unfortunate fact is that, through their selection of the reenactors interviewed and their respective statements and actions, we come away with a grossly distorted image of living historians. Even more disturbing is the fact that controversial statements and unusual opinions included in the film spawn a view that reenactors are odd, unbalanced, bigoted, and superficial. In order to help mend some of the damage done by *The Unfinished Civil War* it is important for reenactors to consider some of the stereotypical and, at best, eccentric perspectives modeled in the film. What follows is a synopsis of some of these unfortunate points of view and the remedies that may be needed to redress the damage done by them.

IT'S A HOBBY NOT A WAY OF LIFE

During the early phases of the film we are introduced to several reenactors who make the most outlandish statements about where reenacting fits into their lives. One Confederate reenactor who, sadly, is prominently featured throughout the film, describes reenacting as "A way of life" that he works to support. In another instance a married couple who are members of a Maryland-based Confederate infantry unit state that "Our entire life centers around reenacting!" Another series of shots captures the almost religious ritual another Maryland reenactor engages in to dress himself prior to going off to "battle." Yes, I too, as a Union reenactor, feel that "The Hobby" has provided me some memorable moments. I strive to have those "magic moments" when some part of my readings and study of the past come together with present day experiences to move me. However, this is a recreational endeavor that is not very important in the great scheme of things. When we dress up our hobbies or interests with larger than life implications we begin to impress others as strange zealots rather than people with a unique interest and something to share.

SLAVERY HAD SOMETHING TO DO WITH THE WAR

At one point the producer, Seth Isler, asks a Confederate reenactor who portrays an Arkansas officer and his wife what they think slavery had to do with the causation of the Civil War. As is all too common among reenactors, these two people then went on to self-assuredly declaim that slavery was a non-factor in the starting of the war. As if this type of shoddy historical "study" is not bad enough these two individuals then went on to state that slaves were "taken care of" and the African-Americans had a better quality of life in the Antebellum era than now. In an amazingly wooden headed manner these blithely stated points of view help to underscore the sometimes held belief you must be a racist to recreate a Confederate impression. By believing, as far too many reenactors do, that slavery was not a major cause of the Civil War, we fall into a category of superficiality that makes us look foolish to serious students of that era. When statements are made which are racist in nature, by a person in a leadership role in this hobby, it makes us all look like closet "haters."

WE LIVE IN THE UNITED STATES AND THAT IS A GOOD THING

It always surprises me when I go to an event and I hear so much "political" discussion of the ever increasing hazards of "big government." Reenactors who hold to the belief there is some connection between current political problems and those of 1861 often sound like people who wish the final result of the Civil War could somehow be reversed. Unless I missed something, the fact the United

States remains a unified and democratic nation has been a net good for our planet. During *The Unfinished Civil War* we meet people portraying themselves as reenactors who strike political poses that cannot help but offend mainstream viewers. To state John C. Calhoun, one of the sowers of division in our nation's history, was "the greatest statesman to grace the earth" or that the NAACP is and organization of complainers and troublemakers can only label reenactors as bigots. The fact that a number of reenactors chose to attend protest meetings on the steps of the Columbia state capitol building in Confederate uniforms at a time when individuals such as David Duke were speaking and where another speaker talked about "taking out" opponents leads the public to look at us as lunatic fringe "militia men." Yes, we live in a nation within which we have the freedom to follow our respective consciences. However, the way in which several reenactors displayed their ultra-right wing and divisionist perspectives draws into question what sort of folks wear Civil War uniforms and what their real agenda is.

IT'S OK TO WEAR BLUE OR GRAY

So much space has been dedicated in reenacting publications to the controversial topic of galvanizing that it is almost boring. While, even within our hobby, it is not always clear why this issue needs to assume an almost mythical level of discourse it certainly is not one that will be readily understood by the public. Sadly, to most modern Americans the Civil War is a mere glimmer of a distant memory. In an age when the teaching of history is all too often slipshod and superficial reenactors have a rare opportunity to provide a valuable and "hands on" lesson. When reenactors state things like "The only way I'd wear blue was if I was lying in a coffin and they exhumed me!" as one Maryland rebel did in this film we are entering into the world of lingering and unreasoning hatred. This same eccentric fellow also was caught on camera talking about killing Yankees while his girl friend chose to wear a sweatshirt with QUANTRELL boldly emblazoned on its front. Linked to some of the more rabid Confederate battle flag supporters featured in this film this man makes reenactors appear to be odd fellows who are still fighting a war whose outcome was resolved long ago. We really do not need to air this sort of dirty laundry on national television and then hope to be taken seriously by anyone.

REALISM CAN GO TOO FAR

In the not so distant past writings in the Wall Street Journal and Tony Horowitz's *Confederates In The Attic*, and portions of Jane Hamilton's critically acclaimed novel *Disobedience* have all painted reenacting as an unusual endeavor. The fact that some reenactors would choose to soak their brass buttons in urine struck many readers as a strange thing to do in pursuit of authenticity. One need only check out a Civil War reenacting forum on the Internet to see that many mountains can be constructed out of molehills in the area of authenticity in reenacting. However, when a viewer watches this film and sees an otherwise seemingly reasonable living historian talk about how he used to starve himself for five days prior to an event in order to acquire an appropriately gaunt look they will see us as candidates for Prozac. Balance and centeredness are concepts that lie at the heart of many spiritual and philosophical views of the world. We would do well to check ourselves periodically in order to make sure that what we are doing is reasonable and not too extreme.

In closing, *The Unfinished Civil War* strikes this writer as a fascinating but embarrassing production. Even as I write these lines I feel an internal cringing at what impression is wrought by this television show. To see reenactors spouting off in a way that makes us all look like dolts, racists, and morons is offensive. The unfortunate linkage between living history and the controversial flag issue so prominently enfolded into this film also sets our hobby back a few decades. While the contributions of African-American reenactors are presented in a very positive fashion by living historians like Leroy Martin of Chicago and Joe McGill of the 54th MA and preservation is well handled by Rob Hodge the net effective of this film is awful. In point of fact, on the day after the airing of *The Unfinished Civil War* I was still getting sarcastic questions from my non-reenacting family members who have always seen my commitment to "The Hobby" as off centered.

In the face of publicity like that which is offered in this Greystone Communications production it behooves each reenactor to take a little time to figure out public relations damage control we can do to better educate the public about what we do and why we do it. In this sense *The Unfinished Civil War* may be a clarion call to the broader reenacting community to reflect on our hobby and how it may appear to outside viewers. We show little respect to those soldiers, both blue and gray, as well as civilians who experienced the tragic moments of the Civil War when we mouth ignorant statements, model intolerance, or encourage hatred. When the war ended in 1865 the people who fought and endured it set about the very difficult task of re-building the nation we now live in. We dishonor their memory by turning a deeply meaningful recreational pursuit into a laughable conglomeration of ignorance and prejudice. Hopefully these lessons can be learned and the embarrassment of this film can serve as a point of growth for all of us.

- Chapter 3 -

TEN CHARACTERISTICS OF SERVANT LEADERSHIP: A GUIDE FOR OFFICERS & NCO'S

In 1964, after a thirty-eight year career in management with AT&T, Robert K. Greenleaf retired. During his many years as an administrator in a major corporation Greenleaf had ample opportunity to hone his skills and beliefs in the domain of leadership. Upon retirement from a very successful and hierarchical organization Greenleaf began a synthesis process in hopes of refining his experiences into a more holistic philosophy of leadership. Through these efforts he came to found the Center for
Applied Ethics that ultimately was renamed the Robert K. Greenleaf Center, an organization that still is actively involved in the study of successful leadership. The keynote theme in Greenleaf's post-retirement work, and that of his adherents, rests in the concept of "Servant Leadership" a mode of operation that appears to have wide applicability in the world of schools.
      Centered on core values that emphasize connection, commitment, and service Greenleaf's schema points toward many of the organizational issues that confront officers and NCO's serving in Civil War living history organizations. At a time when "political" factors are often cited as negative issues affecting the stability of Civil War reenactment units and umbrella organizations it may be wise to review some of the key elements of servant leadership. In looking at

Greenleaf's paradigm one is struck by both his generosity of spirit and the general applications that officers, NCO's, and other formal and informal reenactor leaders can make of the most basic points. What follows are the ten elemental characteristics of a servant leader drawn from Greenleaf's work and potential connections to unit leaders. In reading these points take a few minutes to reflect upon their relevance and the degree to which they fit your own reenacting leadership role and style. Through this reflection and potential synthesis you may find out a great deal about yourself and those who you serve.

1. **Persuasion:** In a traditional organization leaders control subordinates in a top-down manner. Decision-making is a strict prerogative of the "leader" who determines what will happen most specifically because of authority derived from position rather than expertise. A servant leader emphasizes persuasion rather than control in decision-making circumstances. The development of true consensus becomes a hallmark of a servant leader. Servant leaders attempt to convince others rather than control them. This particular element represents one of the sharpest contradictions between servant leadership and traditional hierarchical thinking. In the pseudo-military world of reenacting where people "serve" at their discretion, tyrannical leaders will swiftly find themselves with very few recruits or a constant changing or the guard. Work with people rather than yelling at them and driving them away.
2. **Awareness:** A servant leader strives to find out what people think about a given circumstance. Through finding out the lay of the land a servant leader is secure enough to face criticism and shape future actions due to reasonable feedback. Unlike more control-oriented leaders, servant leaders want to become aware of the root issues involved in any significant action or decision. For

example, if a scenario at an event is totally messed up, check with the troops and find out what they think went wrong. This type of involvement from the ranks will assure greater openness and loyalty.
3. **Healing:** Seldom do traditional or autocratic organizations attend to the inner needs of workers. It is a sad truth that "bosses" can be insensitive to the needs of their employees. If this notion was untrue there would not be so many stereotypically bad bosses in movies, books, television shows, and a host of other media. A servant leader realizes that he or she owes a healing touch to those whom they work with. When people are in pain they need nurturance. A servant leader both helps, and thereby gains personally, through finding opportunities to model compassion with others. If a new recruit is awkward at drill, or a veteran seems burned out, take some time and see what's going on. If you sense that unit members are hurting either physically or mentally check out what is going on. Be connected to the members and they will respect you.
4. **Empathy:** Servant leaders seek to understand and support the people they work with. They have a fundamental belief that other people can be trusted. Only when such faith is clearly violated does a servant leader reject the actions of another person. In those situations it is the behavior and not the core self of the other person that is rejected and judged. Even in the most challenging circumstances a servant leader does not personalize criticism or behavior. The fact that every other person is a unique individual is never completely lost sight of. By being empathetic with the soldiers or civilians in your unit you will develop bonds of trust and commitment that will make everyone's reenacting experience much more satisfying. If members are having problems seek them out and sincerely try to help them.

5. **Conceptualization:** All leaders are confronted with day-to-day problems. It is all too easy to be drawn into a constant stream of fires to put out. While such problems present themselves to servant leaders they also demonstrate the ability to think in a long-term manner as well. Servant leaders realize that for an organization, and the individuals who make up its structure, to thrive it is essential to have creative ideas. Such creativity and conceptualization keeps an organization alive and motivates its members to feel commitment and growth. A reenactment group that lacks a philosophy, focus, and standard of operation will confuse its members. This lack of a shared purpose leads to fragmentation and bad feelings. Seek out or create unique reenacting opportunities in order to keep the members charged up about coming out in the field.
6. **Foresight:** True servant leaders realize that the problems of tomorrow are solved today. They do not wait for opportunities to be reactive and punitive. Instead they exercise foresight to head off problems and develop solutions. They do this complex task through harnessing the strength of those they serve and offering direction that is viewed as everyone's idea. Servant leaders understand the lessons of history, present day applications, and the trends of the future. Stay ahead of the curve by being in touch with major trends in reenacting. Be aware of the better events and opportunities for your unit. Stay in touch with your members and keep things fun.
7. **Stewardship:** For Greenleaf, and other servant leaders, each leader has a responsibility to help direct their organization in a manner that allows for human growth in a responsible manner. Dedicated living historians hold their position in trust. Having a good time in a recreational pursuit is fine and dandy but living historians should have a sense of both history and

preservation. Stewardship infers taking responsibility for something bigger than yourself. A reenactor serving as a leader demonstrates this skill when he or she is able to work with others to make history come alive or when they commit to preservation activities. Such stewardship is a characteristic of a charitably minded person dedicated to servant leadership.

8. **Commitment to the Growth of People:** For a servant leader every person they work with has innate value. This intrinsic value extends beyond their contact with the leader as worker, parent, student, or customer. Each person is important as is his or her growth and development. The servant leader's task is to be available to help in that growth process whenever possible. Good officers or NCO's take the time necessary to assure that new members feel supported, trained, and accepted. People in the unit who have new interests are encouraged rather than driven out. Individuals who want to alter or expand their impressions are listened to and supported. A servant leader accepts and encourages the growth of their colleagues. Living historians in leadership roles who ignore this element of their job will lose members and be seen as aloof.

9. **Building Community:** We live in a world wherein social change may create a steadily deepening sense of isolation. In an era when community is a more difficult concept to define and feel it is important for leaders to help develop positive cultures within the organizations they lead. Reenactment groups are truly effective when there is a sense of shared mission, purpose, and focus. Such community building is an inherent trait of a servant leader. An officer who helps to establish and maintain a shared unit vision will attract and retain members. A leader who is unclear on the concept of unit purpose or who is merely pursuing an ego trip will not keep unit members for long.

10. **Listening:** The art of listening is a skill that many people talk about but few have mastered. Most people realize when another person is listening to them but have difficulty replicating this experience. The ability to be open to the moment and connect with another human being through active listening is a quality that servant leaders consistently model. Active listening also refers to reading not only the spoken words of others but also their feeling tone, non-verbal messages, and unstated needs. Good listeners are sought out by people and hence are provided multiple opportunities for input. To be a good listener requires patience, commitment, compassion, and an inner control. Good listeners also should seek out opportunities for reflection on not only what they have heard but what they are feeling as well. Officers who cannot be approached due to their haughtiness or who are so egocentric that they cannot see anyone's viewpoint but their own will quickly be uncovered for what they are. Poor officers breed poor units. They then cannot see their own mistakes because they will not listen to anybody else's opinion.

In closing, these ten characteristics of servant leadership certainly are relevant to the tasks involved in being an officer of any sort. Sadly, it is all too common for units to fracture over issues that can be traced back to flawed leadership. Units rise, grow, and subside. However, high quality organizations seem to be able to muster satisfied participants for a number of years. How do some groups function in the reenacting field for so long? What makes one unit more resilient than another? In many instances the answer to these questions comes from the quality of the formal and informal leaders in those groups.
If you have served on the field with an officer who not only understood drill and tactics but human nature as

well, you realize that those people make the living history experience a 'magic moment'. In opposing situations, potentially wonderful events can become drudgery when the weekend revolves around power plays, arguments, addlepated commands, and anger. During the Civil War people such as Lee, Grant, Lincoln, and Clara Barton took the concept of service and dedication seriously. They took responsibility for their people and the decisions they had to make. Through these practices they came to be viewed as servant leaders who made a significant difference in their nation's history. Hopefully, through reflecting on these characteristics we can draw upon the resources inherent in each of us to create an atmosphere of purpose, enjoyment, and shared responsibility. Such a positive leadership profile will help bolster interest and participation in our hobby. A failure to follow this pathway may lead to alienation and fragmentation. That kind of negative result hurts the hobby, lessens the experiences of unit members, and can often be traced back to its source—poor leadership.

- Chapter 4 -

RACISM: AN ISSUE FOR LIVING HISTORIANS

Over the past decade it has been my pleasure and privilege to take part in living history aimed at the Civil War era. In that time I have met some wonderful people who share a passion for a time period that continues to exert an affect upon our society. The events, colleagueship, emotion, and education involved in reenacting have become a major part of my life. People not involved in our hobby do not understand how deeply it can grab your spirit and move you.

However, in recent years I have noticed a disturbing trend. Issues of racism seem to crop up with greater frequency than in the past. While I am not a bleeding heart liberal I do consider racism and attendant bigotry to be one of the gravest social issues confronting our nation. While in the ranks as a reenactor it disturbs me to see evidence of such mean spiritedness. In some cases the overt nature of racism struck me as clearly offensive. In other instances people acting in "first person" have engaged in the use of racially charged language under the auspices of being in character for the mid 19th century. In one case individuals portraying Federal soldiers sang authentic period songs inclusive of terms derogatory to African-Americans within the range of hearing of a USCT unit and spectators.

Each of the incidents described above can be explained in a number of ways. Obviously, the racial climate in 1861-65 was much different than the present age. However, even though we, as Civil War reenactors and living historians, strive to recapture the feeling of that bygone age we need to be aware of the fact that we live in an age when diversity and sensitivity to racial issues is essential. In order to balance these needs some compromises need to be made in how we act and react to other reenactors and the public. The suggestions below are aimed at achieving a balance of authenticity and appropriateness in handling racial issues at events.

DO NOT USE RACIAL EPITHETS

Obvious though it may be it is seemingly necessary to mention this first factor. Yes, terms we now associate with racial denigration were quite common in the 1860's. African-Americans were typically referred to with a variety of terms each of which was considered part of the common speech of that time period. A person fully immersed in his or her character as a living historian would probably have considered such terms part of common speech. Many Americans of the Civil War era were, what we would consider, overtly racist. Even many individuals who opposed slavery were in no way liberal by modern standards in terms of their thoughts about Blacks. Therefore, an authentic impression in many cases would encompass attitudes that we now see as abhorrent.

Even though the people of the 1860's were very set in their thought patterns regarding race there is no need to use terms which, in our age, are both offensive and damaging. It is irrelevant to a member of the public who overhears the use of racially charged language that the person eliciting it is "in character". What the listener will understand is that the person using said language is a racist or a lout. The fact that a person is in "first person" or in the zone of their impression will not be understood by most people. Therefore, simply do not use language that will cause people pain and then attempt to defend such actions by dressing it up as "period authentic". The times that I have heard individuals use racial epithets in the ranks or at events has left me with a feeling that the person in question was either an overt racist or a thoughtless fool. Sponsoring sites or organizations will not look kindly upon reenactors if they are confronted by justifiably angered participants or spectators who claim, "All those reenactors are a bunch of racists!" Do we really need this type of publicity? Is our purpose to educate or to shock? Is being in first person a reality or an excuse for indulging in overt acts of racism?

EXPLAIN ATTITUDES THEN AND NOW

When speaking to the public or engaging in school/community presentations take some time to discuss racial attitudes in the 1860's. It is almost too apparent to state that the issues of slavery, emancipation, and subsequent reconstruction continue to live on with us in our present society. There is great good that can come out of tracing the history of these issues for children and adults as we present as living historians. Letting people know how African-Americans were treated and viewed by both Union and Confederate soldiers and civilians can be a huge eye opener for modern day listeners. As living historians with some depth of knowledge in this particular time period we have an opportunity and responsibility to describe how the era that we study contributes to the age within which we live. The issue of race is one that all too often is ignored or not discussed because people are uncomfortable with it. That issue cannot be ignored when talking about the decade within which slavery was debated, fought over, destroyed, and then reinvented in a way under the heading of share-cropping, Jim Crowism, and segregation. So, dive into the topic but do so in a way that is based upon an understanding of the issues as they existed in the past and how they continue in the present.

UNDERSTAND YOUR OWN VIEW OF THE QUESTION

     A reflective person is better able to teach others about a topic. By looking within yourself and assessing your own abilities, feelings, and attitudes one can be better able to come to grips with serious matters. A reenactor who does not understand the effects of race and slavery on that time period is really not coming to grips with one of, if not the most important, factors which resulted in the carnage of 1861-65. Slavery as the cause of the Civil War is often debated around campfires at events. That topic is one that can be interpreted in a variety of ways. Yet, it would be difficult to presume to have any depth of knowledge of the Civil War time frame without having some grasp of slavery as a significant social and political component of both the antebellum south and the war itself. Be able to articulate a reasoned view of slavery and its role in igniting the terrible swift sword of war across our nation. If you feel that slavery was not the paramount cause of the coming of war be able to explain why that appears true to you. If you see an inherent connection between slavery, and all its attendant evils and corruptions, and the state of conflict be able to articulate a perspective. Take a look inside yourself to assess where you are on this issue. In my own view I find it difficult to imagine that our people would have slaughtered one another to the cost of over 600,000 dead without the concerns that flowed out of the slavery issue. You may have a diametrically different view of this question. Think about it and bring your thoughts to bear on your presentation and impression.

DO NOT IGNORE RACISM

Earlier in this piece I mentioned three separate instances where racism, or apparent racism, occurred at an event. Each of these examples is based upon personal experience and each engendered challenges to those who observed or overheard what transpired. When ugliness comes into view it is easy to look away or pretend to not observe it. When a reenactor engages in racially charged behavior it can be unpleasant to confront it. We are not law enforcement agents. We generally are not charged with maintaining the general order and decorum of an event. Yet, we are all responsible for the impression an event, scenario, or our hobby in general casts out to the public. How should you react when situations of a racially offensive nature occur around you?

In my own experience the case where a fellow reenactor used racial epithets in ranks left me feeling conflicted. On the one hand I could not ignore it. On the other, I kept thinking, "I'm in a ersatz group and will never see these people again. Why not ignore it and slip away?" In the end I did speak to the person in question and told him that what he was saying was rude and offensive. Although he did not handle this information very well he did desist from making any more comments. Ignoring a wrong does not benefit anyone. If you are in a situation similar to the one I described only you can assess what you need to do. However, looking the other way acts to authorize that person's actions.

In a second instance the singing of Kingdom Come resulted in a cause celebre at an event in Naperville, Illinois. In that case the use of the period authentic lyrics by a group of Federal infantrymen caused offense to both park officials and participants. What followed was some highhandedness on the part of many participants and a subsequent eviction of the involved unit. This eviction was followed by a "walkout" on the part of several other Federal units in support of the perceived unfairness to the other Federals. I arrived the morning of the hubbub with my six-year-old with no intention other than to spend the day in uniform with my son and watch the event with the medical staff. However, what confronted me was a political event rotating around issues related to perceived racism. My own unit was leaving as part of the "walkout" but I had mixed feelings about the situation. I had observed reenactors using racial epithets prior to the battle the previous day in circumstances wherein the public did overhear them. Those individuals defended their actions by defining their words as part of their first person. Still, there was more going on than just the singing of one particular Civil War song. Therefore, after thinking about the situation, and reflecting upon the circumstances, I decided to participate with another Federal unit. It just seemed wrong to let the paying public down in a situation where the lines of responsibility were unclear. Also, by "walking out" what were we defending? Issues of racism are sometimes obscured by "political" agendas. When confronted by such a situation try to make an individual decision and not be dragged along by peer pressure or fear.

In closing, while I believe the vast majority of reenactors handle themselves very well with the public there are situations which arise which can be offensive. One of those types of negative circumstances involves racial misunderstanding or prejudice. Instances do occur where the direct or indirect actions of reenactors can cause others to be racially offended. We need to remember that the demeanor and actions that we project to the public and our fellow reenactors exerts a direct affect upon them. We are each responsible for our actions. We can choose to act in a responsible manner or not. Those individuals or groups who, in the name of authenticity, allow or condone the use of racially charged language cross the line into offensiveness. Others who choose to ignore such actions not only abet the perpetrators but also sell our hobby short in the eyes of others. Try to balance the truth of the 19th century with the realities of this age. To do otherwise will lead to ill will and misunderstanding.

- Chapter 5 -

STRATEGIES FOR REENACTORS TO AVOID "BURNOUT"

For many reenactors the beginning of a new "season" starts in early spring. Company drills, early season events, and living histories at the start of the reenacting year are filled with an enthusiasm that bespeaks the end of winter. Putting on the "wools" at the start of the year is both easy and fulfilling. Yet, as July and August roll around a variety of factors can lead to the proverbial "burnout". Additionally, if a reenactor has been involved in the hobby for any length of time the burnout factor can begin to weigh heavily. The burst of springtime bravado may be replaced by a feeling that reenacting is not only no longer fulfilling but rather a chore. Without some attention to burnout a reenactor might lose interest in the hobby and then drop out. In order to avoid this scenario and offer some helpful hints what follows are some tips gleaned from personal experience that might help avoid burning out.

Quality versus Quantity: There is always a tendency to over commit to events. It is very easy to say yes to one of your pards when he says "Hey, let's go do the event over at Slippery Rock; I hear it's a blast". While the annual Slippery Rock event may be a "blast" it also might well be more of the same. Be careful to identify the type and number of events you can handle. The depth of your living history experiences may well be more valuable to you than the number of events you can cram into one season. Search within yourself and find the type of experiences you most enjoy in this hobby. Set your annual schedule of events up so that those peak experiences are what you go out for.

Do Parts of Events: In many cases it is possible to come out for part of a weekend and participate in a scaled down manner. For example, if there are work and family pressures that preclude spending a whole weekend at an event go out for Saturday only. Participate in as committed a way as you can and then go home. Every event need not contain camping Friday and Saturday with a full schedule of events across the weekend. A taste of an event may give you the experience you are looking for without creating family tension or frustration.

Bring Only What You Need: There are many depths and levels to reenacting. The level of commitment felt by progressives, hardcores, mainstream participants, and permutations in between vary. However, a sure pathway to exhaustion is to make a hobby into a logistical nightmare. By bringing too much gear and odds and ends the weekend can become work rather than pleasure. When the weather turns bad and you are forced to remove all your stuff from a site it will not be fun. Establish the least common denominator you need to make it through an event and then cut back even more. What you will find is that "less is more".

Know Your Limits: People often try to do too much. If you are hot or tired in a scenario take a hit or fall out. If you are really not up for the skirmish be an early casualty. Try to know your physical and mental limits. You do not need to be at every drill, tactical, dress parade, and event. It is a hobby and not the real military. By pushing too hard you endanger yourself and those around you. Also, by making a wonderful recreational activity into a grind you rob it of the value that probably drew you to it in the first place.

Maintain Personal Wellness: You will not enjoy a hobby that has physical activity as part and parcel of it if you are not at a reasonable level of fitness. Every reenactor does not have to look like a veritable Rambo. However, if you cannot handle the physical demands find an alternate impression to what you are doing. Exercise, eat well, and come to an event with a level of fitness that will allow you to have fun. If you are falling out on the march or going down with the heat you will not enjoy this hobby. Further, coming onto the field when you know your health may cause a problem is irresponsible. Worrying about the physical demands of a recreational activity will create rather than alleviate stress.

Understand Your Family's Role in the Hobby: Some people are blessed with spouses and children who love reenacting and are active participants. In other cases part of the family participates and enjoys living history while others are supportive but non-participatory. In some instances the reenactor faces tension at home as his or her participation is seen as silly, costly, or divisive. Know where your hobby fits into the family's pattern of needs. The surest way to burnout in a hobby is to have to argue with your spouse or children about their participation. Making others participate in an activity like reenacting against their will leads to misery. Conversely, having to beg or argue to go off by yourself to participate will get tiresome. Understand what is a reasonable level of commitment within your particular family culture. Establish a balance and reassess as needed in order to enhance both your enjoyment of reenacting and your longevity in the hobby.

Diversify Your Impression: Too much of the same thing can lead to boredom and burnout. If you are starting to question why you are an infantryman how about giving another impression some thought? By developing a civilian impression, or one from another branch of the services, you may open up new vistas that help to revitalize your flagging interest. Each impression has its distinct plusses and minuses. Yet, diversity can be the spice of life. Try to recharge your enthusiasm by attempting something different.

Assess What You Are Doing: What is it about reenacting that you most enjoy? Is it the camaraderie you feel with fellow reenactors? Do you really enjoy the educational opportunities that living history provides? Does the camping and travel portion of the hobby stir you? Are you driven to refine your impression to a point that satisfies you? Whatever the reasons for your commitment to a taxing and expensive hobby you must have some compelling reason(s) to be involved. Reflect on what those reasons are and focus your energies in those areas. If, for example, the actual battle reenactments and skirmishes are not of interest to you find living history events, preservation marches, and other activities that center upon the things you find fulfilling. If you seem not to have as much interest in going out onto the filed and would rather write about the time period feel free to do so. Determine what it is that you enjoy about the hobby and do those things.

Avoid Political Issues As Much As Possible: All too often the "political" element is what drives people out of organizations and activities. "Politics" can be a euphemism for ego, narcissism, disagreement, and personality conflict. Unfortunately, people do not always get along and agree. If you find yourself increasingly frustrated by factors that fall into the "political" arena you may also be approaching the burnout phase. In order to avoid this deadfall reflect on whom you are recreating with. If your unit is heading in a direction that you cannot support it may well be time to go off as an "independent" or seek new comrades. If you are involved in a leadership role in a unit and it is wearing you down--give it up. When a few personalities in your group are beginning to grate on you either find ways to avoid them, positively confront them with your irritation, or begin to think about a new home. Political and inter-personal problems within a group will turn a formerly fun filled activity into a battle. Find a place where you fit in comfortably and have a good time.

Be Prepared: The old Boy Scout motto is appropriate for the reenacting community. If you are constantly at the last minute racing to roll rounds, setting up your gear, or figuring out whom you are driving with your enthusiasm for this hobby will eventually be affected. To the greatest extent possible plan ahead what you will need for an event. Know where the event is. Have your gear in order and ready to go. Pack the vehicle as far in advance of departure as is reasonable. Determine who you are riding with and whose vehicle you will be using. Make whatever reservations you need to well in advance. In general, plan your outing in as careful a manner as you can so that you avoid last minute rushing and stress. Anxiety produces stress. Lack of preparation produces anxiety.

Read About What You Are Doing: By reading about the impression you have, the unit you portray, the battle you are going to recreate, or the war in general you deepen your understanding of this time period. By having a firmer grasp on what happened and what people of the 19th century actually experienced you may be better equipped to have longevity in this hobby. For example, reading can provide a sense of purpose when confronted with bad weather, poor food, and other creature discomforts. To know what men and women of the Civil War era lost or sacrificed can help a modern day reenactor learn from the seeming discomforts that we all experience at events.

Remember That Things Change: Be aware that your interest, and that of people in your group, will wax and wane. People and circumstances are constantly changing. An event that was fun for years may shrink down and sputter out. Comrades in your unit move, transfer to other states, or leave the hobby. Your own state of mind shifts and your interests do too. If you feel that "things just aren't what they used to be" you are correct. Be prepared to understand and accept change. If you are less interested in one thing and more so in another that is a natural state of being. Go with the flow, be aware of your attitudes, and let time pass. All too often people make snap decisions based upon information that will change. People quit our hobby for reasons that appear strange but may be deeper seated than we know. By being aware that things change you may be better prepared to accept where you are in your reenacting life.

In closing, 'burning out' in the work force is a common occurrence. Unfortunately, it is also possible to take a leisure activity and transform it into a situation that creates rather than lessens pressures. Civil War reenacting is not immune from the process of burnout. From my own experience in this hobby I realize that my feelings, thoughts, and practices over the past few years are different than they were ten years ago.

By reflecting on the suggestions and situations noted above, hopefully you can assess what you want to do in this wonderful hobby. Reenacting has provided me with a wealth of experiences and opportunities. It has also created some stress in my life. By attempting to maintain a more balanced approach to our hobby I hope it is possible to both enhance and prolong your involvement in it.

- Chapter 6 -

Caring for "Shank's Mare": Tips on How to Maintain Good Foot-care in the Field

During the Fredericksburg campaign of 1862 one New Jersey sergeant encountered some trouble on the march. He had been issued new shoes and they were taxing him dearly. The sergeant's feet were becoming blistered, swollen, and infected. Every time his regiment halted on the march this unfortunate NCO had to remove his shoes and attend to his feet. Each of these painful instances left the troubled man looking at his torn and bloody feet. The infection that had set in left pus mingled with blood in a scabby mess that adhered to his worn socks. When the march renewed fresh scabs and wounds "cut into the raw flesh like a knife." Each step became a punishment for this Civil War soldier as he struggled with a problem that plagued many of his comrades as well as modern-day reenactors.

Nothing can more easily destroy an event than having foot problems. The gnawing irritation of newly blossoming blisters can ruin even the most magic of moments. Just as Civil War soldiers struggled with inadequate footwear, so too do modern living historians. Yet, there are some simple tips that can help reenactors avoid the sad state of affairs that the aforementioned New Jersey unionist experienced.

Marching in Civil War brogans can be a challenge. These cloddish shoes were not designed with all the scientific know-how of modern hiking boots. Brogans offer very little arch support. They are poorly designed in terms toe placement and room for foot expansion brought about by the natural swelling involving in hiking. Civil War shoes also are made of tough materials rather than the padded synthetics of modern era boots. All in all it is easy to see why both Civil War soldiers and modern-day reenactors suffer from minor to severe foot problems if they are in the field marching.

What follows are ten suggestions on how living historians can avoid some of the typical foot problems that can materialize. While these suggestions are in no way biblical in their truth they are based upon many years of experience both as a reenactor and as a backpacker. Hopefully these tips can be of value to folks trying to recreate history without experiencing the pain that foot problems can cause. Remember that it will be exceedingly unlikely that you will enjoy yourself when every stride is a torturous endeavor. Take time to care for your feet and the rewards of your attention will be manifold.

Wear Two pairs of Socks

While it is true that Civil War soldiers minimized their marching kit it is also true that most advice on hiking would call for the wearing of two pairs of socks at one time. The operating principal in operation in this premise is that blistering occurs when repeated friction arises. The rubbing of your foot's skin against socks, shoe leather, or rough spots in the shoe's design will, over time, create enough heat & friction to blister your foot. Wearing an inner, liner sock affords your foot a separate friction barrier that will make blistering much less likely. Long distance hikers generally wear a thin liner sock inside their thicker woolen or composite hiking sock. Civil War purists could choose to simply wear a thinner cotton sock as their liner or two pairs of authentic socks. Less choosy participants could easily pack a few modern liners in their pack and switch them off as the weekend event evolves. Whatever your disposition, the use of two socks is highly recommended as a reasonable preventative measure aimed at eliminating or reducing blisters.

Watch out for Hot Spots

Before a blister forms the skin on your foot will become tender. The initial rubbing should become noticeable long before a blister forms. These "hot spots" are early warning signs that something is not quite right down in your shoe. In many cases people try to ignore or walk through their hot spots. This is a foolish error as when a hot spot exists a blister is likely to follow. If you feel an uncomfortable element in your shoe stop and attend to it. The problem could simply be a bunching of your socks that can easily be attended to. In other cases the hot spot will look like a reddening of your foot. If you notice a discoloration be sure to cover it with moleskin or Band-Aids. Change socks as needed and closely monitor the hot spot. Do not ignore a hot spot or worse problems will follow.

Pace Yourself

Corporal Cort of the 92nd Illinois observed after one grueling march, "Some of the largest and stoutest men were the first to give out while the small ones stuck to it but I find that it is not the phisical (sic) strength but the determination that carries one through a long march." There is no reward for being the fastest marcher or a hero in the reenacting ranks. On the march you need to pace yourself. By trying to do too much you threaten to physically break down. Dangers linked to heat, exhaustion, and overdoing it affect many aspects of a reenactor's health. One additional concern is that by pushing the pace and mileage too far a reenactor runs the risk of breaking down their feet as well as their spirit. Take your time and know what your pace is. If you ignore this reality you could end up like Justis Sullivan of the 17th Connecticut who pushed too hard, blistered his feet, and stated, "my gait was somewhat like that of a lame duck, but I waddled along at first as fast as the remainder of our crew, but toward noon I brought up the rear."

Break in Your Shoes

If you have bought new brogans wear them many times before you take them in the field for any sort of marching. Breaking in shoes is essential unless you wish to risk having a very bad time at your first event. New shoe leather is rather unforgiving to feet. Thus, it is advised to take some walks in your new brogans and wear them in so that they are fit for service. Your brogans will, over time, mold to your feet and become a passable shoe. However, that is not an immediate metamorphosis. Take some time to break in your shoes and dividends of comfort will be paid to you at events. A failure to do so could leave you like one Texas private who wore ill devised shoes and was left with feet that "looked as big as two 20-pound canvas hams."

Rest & Soak Your Feet

When you are done marching, drilling, and campaigning take some time to rest your feet. There is always the temptation after a long day of events to hike on over to the sutlers and shop. If you have had a long day on your feet stop and think for a moment. Would it not be better to stop and sit for a while? You are not really used to wearing even well broken in Civil War shoes. Perhaps it would be better to sit down, get out of your shoes and socks, put your tired feet up, and take a rest. Feet swell after a day's hiking. The compression of hiking will naturally cause swelling. A good strategy at day's end is to soak your feet. If there is a stream or lake near the campsite head on over and plunge your feet into it for a while. Soaking reduces swelling and allows blood flow to return to normal in your feet. You may be amazed at how bracing a foot soaking can be after many miles on your feet. Otherwise, any walking you do may be similar to some experienced by Union veteran Wilbur Fisk who described the last miles of a long day as steps that were "doled out in suffering by inches."

Use Moleskin

Moleskin is a modern intrusion into the Civil War world but it is an invisible one. No one will know if you have strips of moleskin covering your blistered or careworn feet. There is no harm in using modern medical practices at a reenactment. It would be a fanatic indeed who chose to refuse the care of a doctor if he or she broke their leg or suffered heat exhaustion. In the same spirit, why would you balk at using moleskin to assuage the discomfort your feet are experiencing? Moleskin is a wonderful product that is readily available. It can be cut into various shapes and configurations. Some of it is hyper-padded and suitable for the worst blisters. Moleskin is a product that has helped me survive many Civil War events as well as hundreds of trail miles. I swear by it and highly recommend it to you.

Train & Condition Yourself

Civil War soldiers were generally young men who worked tough, physical jobs back home. However, even these hard faced young men suffered on the march. One Civil War veteran recalled tough marches in this way, "Why, I have marched for whole days scarcely noticing even the general lay of the country, because I was too tired. Everything seemed a task. My gun was cutting into my shoulder. My accoutrements felt like great iron bands. My knapsack was a load. The 60 or 120 rounds of cartridges were a dead weight, and my canteen and haversack very cumbersome, as, footsore and weary, sometimes hungry and thirsty, we dragged along." If you want to enjoy reenacting you need to at least minimally condition yourself for the tasks at hand. Foot care is a conditioning activity as well. If you do not want to have foot problems you need to walk. Walking, hiking, jogging, or other physical training will both condition you for the rigors of reenacting while also toughening up your otherwise vulnerable feet.

Treat Blisters

While writing home George A. Bowen, A Rhode Island private, informed his wife, "I'm all right except (for) the doggorned blisters on my feet, and I hope these few lines find you enjoying the same blessings." Now, while Private Bowen probably was not wishing the same blistered fate upon his beloved spouse he was sharing a common compliant of Civil War soldiers. They got blisters and sometimes suffered because of that reality. If you plan on doing much reenacting or hiking you will eventually get blisters. This reality is less important than how you treat blisters once you have them. There is contradictory advice in terms of blister treatment. Some folks suggest simply covering a blister and keeping it clean. Others suggest piercing a blister with a sterile needle or sharps device and then covering it. In this writer's opinion, the optimal treatment is to cover your blister with moleskin or other protective material until you have an opportunity in camp to fully attend to it. Once in camp, carefully puncture and drain the blister. Then cover the area with a Band-Aid that ahs been treated with antiseptic cream. Place a final layer of moleskin over this affair and be sure to wear two dry socks. Be sure to care for the blistered area for a few days until most of the tenderness is gone. If you are going to be in the field for several days, take time every day to tend to you blistered areas. This will be time well spent.

Lighten the Load

If you bring too much gear with you there is a very great likelihood that you will suffer. In a search for greater creature comforts there is always a temptation to bring "just one more thing" with you in the field. However, this type of thinking can, and probably will, lead to too great a pack weight. Pack weight translates to enormous pounding and pressure on your joints and feet. Every extra pound that you stuff into your pack will pound away on your feet with every step. Be stringent in your packing. Bring only what you need for the event. Remember that you really are not a Civil War soldier on the march. If you forget something you can live without it until the end of the weekend. You really are not fully dependent upon the gear you have brought to survive. Therefore, be frugal and sparing in your equipage and your feet will thank you.

Stress Functionality & Not Appearance

Lieutenant Henry Dwight of the 20th Ohio saw some rough service during his tour of duty. Thinking back to his days in camp and on the march Dwight recalled the rigors of the field, "The most elegant dress uniform will become torn and spotted, and the brightly polished boots will become soiled with mud when one is reduced to marching in line of battle through swamps, thickets and briar patches, and then sleeping night after night on the bare ground with only heaven's clouds as an overcoat." A veteran's gear was judged worthy or not by how it served its owner and not how shiny it was. One Civil War veteran lamented over boots that looked fine but "wore the ends of my toenails down to the quick, blistered my feet, and (made) them sore generally." Your gear, inclusive of your boots, must serve you well. It is better to have effective gear than anything that may look great but which wears badly. Over time you need to make sure that all of your accoutrements are purposeful, authentic, and comfortable. Nowhere is this truism more important than in the area of shoes.

Conclusion

Civil War soldiers quickly learned the lessons that marching will teach you. If you over pack, under train, walk recklessly, lack dry socks, and fail to attend to foot injuries you will suffer. Wilbur Fisk, a Vermont veteran, remembered seeing another poor infantryman with "one boot in one hand, and the other stuck on his gun, while his stockings were nearly worn off his feet by the dirt and hard traveling. His feet were swelled and he had several large blisters on them. He was a new recruit, and one of the veterans asked him how much of his town bounty he had paid for that day." Unless you are open to the same experience of this hapless recruit you need to learn the lessons taught to us by both history and experience. A soldier, or a reenactor, cannot march well if his feet are betrayed. Therefore, taking care of Shank's Mare, as foot travel was referred to in the 19th century, is an essential survival skill that every reenactor should learn. To fail to do so is to risk both pain and disillusion.

Sources

Gregory Coco, *The Civil War Infantryman: In Camp, on the March, and in Battle,*
 (1996), Gettysburg, PA: Thomas Publications.

Wilbur Fisk, *Hard Marching Every Day: The Civil War Letters of Private Wilbur Fisk,*
 (1992), Lawrence, KS: The University Press Kansas.

James I. Robertson, Jr., *Soldiers Blue and Gray,* (1988) Columbia, SC: The University of
 South Carolina Press.

- Chapter 7 -

ARTILERY SAFETY: A REENACTING CASE STUDY

In September 1997, the life on one reenactor was permanently changed by an accident on the field. His name was Rod Bulley, and he still carries the physical scars he received when things went wrong with the cannon he was using to recreate a Civil War battle. Rod was a cannoneer with the Baltimore Light Artillery at the time of his accident. He had been an artillery reenactor for about five years. His wife, Gayle, and their six children had also been participants in the living history events of the Baltimore Light Artillery. Rod's interest in reenacting was the result of a lifetime of reading about the Civil War as well as being intrigued by the events he had attended as a spectator. The artillery unit Rod came to join was a small Confederate battery with a limited membership and one 12-Pounder Mountain Howitzer. Because of low membership, the Baltimore Light often had to solicit volunteers from other units to fill out the gun crew for events.

The unit's Mountain Howitzer was the property of the battery commander and was manufactured in the 1960's. Mountain Howitzers being smaller in scale than their larger counterparts such as Napoleons, 3" Ordnance Rifles, 10-Pounder Parrotts, or 6-pounder Field Guns were more awkward to serve. The smaller size of the gun does not allow the forward two crewmen, working position 1 & 2, to handle their duties in the more secure space between the tube and the wheel. Instead, the Numbers 1 & 2 men have to work from outside the wheels and thus are forced to reach and expose themselves to more potential damage at the gun's bore. Yet, with appropriate drill and practice, Rod and his colleagues in the Baltimore Light Artillery were confident no mishaps could occur. These feelings of confidence were to be shattered at the *Civil War Train Raid* held near Gettysburg in September 1997.

A local landowner, the Gettysburg Scenic Railway, and several reenacting groups hosted the *Train Raid*. The event occurred twice yearly during one weekend in July and another in September and had been in operation for about a decade. Rod's unit had been participating for five years and, as the sole artillery piece, they were one of the center stage elements of the event.

The structure of the *Train Raids* was almost always the same. Twice each day, on Saturday and Sunday, a 19th century steam engine drew passengers and Federal infantry along the railway. At a designated point along the route the Baltimore Light were to fire a round. At that point the train was to stop, the Federals were to disembark, and a small skirmish ensued between the Union troops and Confederate forces hiding in the woods. After the skirmish, which typically involved the Baltimore Light firing about three rounds, the train ride continued on down the line and back.

The railroad offered reduced fares to reenactors and their families and provided a small stipend to each participant. Ticket prices for regular passengers were raised for those two weekends to offset these expenses. The event was normally one of the most profitable weekends of the year for the Railway and was an enjoyable experience for the participating reenactors.

However, in 1997 there were some seemingly minor alterations in the event script. The time for off-loading the Union infantrymen was slightly compressed. The opposing forces were to be brought into combat slightly more quickly. The number of artillery rounds to be fired was increased. Individually, each of these changes seemed insignificant. Collectively, the changes contributed to a disastrous accident that was to maim one person.

Rod and his wife arrived on the event Sunday. Rod had expected to be joined by his eldest son who also participated with the unit but the lad was not in attendance when the setup for the morning skirmish began. The Baltimore Light was shorthanded and forced to recruit two volunteers to man the gun. With two new men drawn from an infantry and dismounted cavalry unit, and a five-man crew, the Baltimore Light set out to take the field and participate in the show.

Rod was in the Number 1 position at the right front of the gun. This position involves wet sponging the tube and ramming home each round. The gun owner, and unit leader, was in the Number 3 position with responsibility for thumbing the vent and using the priming wire to prick the charge. The remaining veteran cannoneer was placed in the Number 4 position and handled the friction primers and lanyard. One of the two inexperienced recruits was placed on the limber box and served as a powder runner. The remaining novice was assigned the Number 2 posting with a responsibility for worming the piece and loading rounds— one of the most critical jobs on the gun.

Rod was wary of working the front of the gun with an inexperienced partner. Worming can be a demanding task and even experienced artillerists sometimes struggle with the requirements of the Number 2 position. The Number 2 man is responsible for using the corkscrew-like worm to remove smoldering remains from the tube. In 19th century gunnery these remains could be part of the sacking materials used to contain the powder charge. In modern day reenacting the wormer is charged with extracting the aluminum foil used to mold the charge. An inexperienced Number 2 man might leave trace elements of this smoldering material and set up a dangerous situation. This situation can then lead to a cannoneer's worst nightmare—the premature ignition of a round. During the skirmish Rod noted that the Number 2 man was having difficulty accomplishing his job. Several times Rod had to direct the man to "go down the barrel again" when he was dissatisfied with his work and what he was seeing.

Prior to going onto the field the Baltimore Light Artillery had prepared their rounds for battle. According to common practice among artillerists and the National Park Service, a maximum charge for a 4.62" 12-Pounder Mountain Howitzer is six ounces of black powder. The typical round size used by the Baltimore Light Artillery was eight. On the day of the September 1997 *Train Raid* the rounds were being made with ten ounces of black powder and were then topped off with several ounces of flour to augment the flash and smoke of each blast. This practice of using flour is discouraged by artillerists as it burns at a much different rate than powder. This differential in combustion can result in smoldering flour being forced into any irregularities within a gun barrel where they can pose a hazard when subsequent rounds are rammed home. Flour can also clump after it leaves the barrel thereby becoming a projectile dangerous to anyone downfield.

During the event Rod was also troubled by the rate of fire. The crew was working at a faster pace than normally they would. Generally, the crew would fire three rounds during the skirmish scenario and then withdraw to the Confederate infantry line. In 1997 the crew was asked to fire five or six rounds in the same time frame. This increased rate of fire created greater pressure on the gun crew as well as lessening the time between rounds and enhancing the possibility of error.

All things considered, at the conclusion of the morning skirmish, Rod was troubled. He had lunch and replayed the morning's events. Rod was worried about the rate of fire and how close the infantry had come to the gun. He was also awaiting the arrival of his son whom he hoped would replace the novice Number 2 man whose performance troubled Rod. Rod considered passing on the afternoon scenario and joining his wife as a spectator. With these fears, Rod contemplated approaching the gun commander and "stepping down" for the second raid. But, the crew was already shorthanded and if Rod stepped down they would have trouble manning the piece. There was not much time before the second skirmish was to commence and Rod buried his fears. Rod still hoped that things would work out all right and, hence, he rejoined the crew.

When the gun crew approached the piece for the afternoon skirmish the commander informed them that they would each maintain the same positions for that scenario. This decision surprised Rod because typically crewmembers were rotated to different roles for each skirmish. Rod thought it might be wise to move one of the veteran members to the Number 2 position and relieve the novice volunteer. This man could be given the less responsible job of handling the lanyard in the Number 4 position. However, as the event unfolded Rod and each man on the gun was in the same slot they had filled in the morning.

As the train arrived at the battlefield the Baltimore Light Artillery fired its first round. Rod worked away ramming the first three rounds home. As he began to ram a fourth round down the gun disaster struck. When Rod started to ram that round home it prematurely went off. The ramrod was blown out of the barrel with pieces of it flying down range toward the approaching Federal infantrymen— and destroying Rod Bulley's right hand in the process. Distant witnesses later said that they knew something was wrong because the sound of the ignition as different from what they had heard before.

The force of the blast blew away the middle three fingers of Rod's right hand as well as damaging his thumb and pinkie. There was additional damage to his arm and shoulder as well as shock and pain. The thumb of the Number 3 man was dislocated and he received flash burns to his face. As Rod writhed on the ground bystanders came forward to give him medical attention. Finally Rod was taken to a nearby hospital for more in depth initial treatment.

A momentary accident had caused permanent physical disability. As a microbiologist responsible for specimen preparation, the loss of much of one hand had a direct effect on Rod Bulley's ability to do his work and support a family. Pain was to plague him for years. Additionally, the adjustment to Rod's injuries was a difficult one for him and his family. Surgeries, medical bills, anger, grief, and doubt all combined to make Rod's injuries difficult to bear. Still, lessons can be learned from Rod's experiences that may be very valuable to modern day artillery reenactors.

LESSONS TO BE LEARNED

DRILL: In the 1860's it was essential that every member of a gun crew become knowledgeable and adept at all positions on the piece. Issues of battlefield attrition, illness, and leaves made it important that each cannoneer know what to do should they be called upon to fulfill a role not generally their specialty. Ten years ago, when this writer entered into the field of Civil War reenacting as an artillerist there were great inconsistencies among various batteries as per drill and its application. Each artillery group utilized somewhat different hand and body positions during the loading and clearing of the piece. Equipment standards varied across units, as did the numbering system for the crew positions. Additionally, the size of rounds, powder charges, means of rolling rounds, powder grades, firing rates, and firing commands were far from uniform. Regional differences were also pronounced. Artillery units from the East, South, Midwest, and Trans-Mississippi areas all seemed to have differing approaches to drill and safety making it difficult to come together and develop a "best practices" mode of operation. All of these factors created opportunities for misunderstanding and mishap.

Today there is an emerging consensus as to what should be incorporated into standard drill and practice. There has been a steady movement toward greater consistency in the vital area of safety. The work of the founding members of the Fort Niagara Artillery School, the North-South Skirmish Association, the National Park Service, and various artillery certification groups have created a common ground among artillerists that was previously absent. Such growing consistency of safe practice grounded upon the lessons learned by our Civil War predecessor's leaves far less room for disastrous error.

With greater consistency of drill comes a more universal approach to safety, making accidents such as the one experienced by Rod Bulley extremely uncommon. If the now more generally accepted components of drill had been in operation during the September 1997 *Train Raid*, Mr. Bulley's accident probably would not have occurred. These components include:

1. Only experienced and well-drilled crewmembers should work in the Number 1 & 2 positions.
2. Rounds shall not exceed maximum size recommendations.
3. The rate of fire should not exceed one round in three minutes.
4. Firing should never occur in a confined area or when infantry, other service branches, or spectators as near at hand.
5. Flour should not be used as a "chaser" element for blast enhancement.

SAFETY OFFICERS: Another area that has evolved over the past decade is the involvement of safety officers at events. Due to liability concerns and safety issues, participants, organizers, and event sponsors need to take whatever precautions they reasonably can to avoid accidents. Rather than relying upon a "self-policing" approach whereby reenactors monitor their own needs the use of a safety inspector is a much more reasoned approach. Because of the inherent dangers of artillery, having a safety officer for that branch of service, regardless of the size of the event, is just common sense.

    The artillery safety officer should be an individual skilled and knowledgeable in the area of Civil War era weaponry and its use in reenacting. The safety officer needs to be responsible for making sure that each cannon, limber, caisson, and all equipment are thoroughly inspected. The National Park Service has developed a standard checklist to assure that the artillery piece and its accoutrements are up to safety standards. A careful examination of a cannon may reveal cracks or pitting in the barrel that might contribute to harboring sparks and thereby cause a premature ignition of a charge. A safety officer should also check the quality of the sponge and rammers to make sure they fit the piece well and are in workable condition. The upkeep of the carriage and limber can be monitored to assure that the piece in a field-ready state of being. In general, the gun and supporting equipment can be checked to assure that they are fit and ready to be used.

A safety officer can put the crew through its paces via the drill or observe them being drilled by their own officers. Such an approach can reveal the general competence of each crew and its respective members. If this had been done at the 1997 *Train Raid* it is probable that the situation that led up to Mr. Bulley's wounding could have been averted. A novitiate cannoneer would not have been allowed to remain in a keynote position while veteran crewmembers held less responsible postings. Also, during such a drill the safety officer could examine rounds. If, as was the case in Rod Bulley's experience, the rounds were too large or made in an impermissible fashion the crew could have been told to remake them or be banned from the scenario. The use of additives such as flour could have been discovered and that ill-advised practice halted.

All too often there has been a tendency in the reenacting world to rely upon the common sense and skill of crews to monitor themselves. While most artillerists have a firm knowledge of drill, safety procedures, and best practices this is not always the case. Simply owning a cannon does not make a person an expert in artillery practices. There are commonly accepted safety procedures that each gun crew needs to be held accountable for. An impartial safety officer—a person who is held solely accountable for oversight of that critical element of a well-run event—is a sound investment of personnel in any living history situation.

In many instances, this practice is already in place. Where it is not, organizers are urged to rethink this gap in service and strongly consider using a safety officer. Such a move might well save injury or potential death.

SPONSORSHIP: Individuals or groups thinking about sponsoring an event should carefully consider the possibility of a serious accident. Rod Bulley's injuries resulted in a lawsuit ultimately settled at the Federal Court level in Harrisburg, Pennsylvania in the year 2000. This writer was called upon to participate in that case as an expert witness and would prefer never to have such an opportunity based upon another person's pain again. To avoid such a drastic chain of events sponsors must pay close attention to safety issues.

As already noted, the use of an expert responsible for monitoring safety is a good first step. The size of an event will not matter in a court of law if suit is brought against you or your organization due to the maiming of a person or people. It will be a poor defense to state that, yes it is common knowledge that larger events use written registration packets inclusive of expansive safety guidelines—but no, it did not seem necessary to follow this practice at your, smaller, event. In the face of a life threatening and disabling accident, the absence of such standard procedures will leave the sponsor(s) exposed to potential or actual liability.

To host or sponsor an event where hundreds or thousands of people are going to discharge black powder weaponry is to invite risk. Prudent risk management is more assured if basic safety procedures and standards are published, provided to all participants, and enforced. The failure to adhere to such an approach invites litigation. Merely having the reenactors sign a piece of paper representing a waiver of responsibility does not hold water if the sponsors then hold an event where basic safety guidelines are ignored or unenforced. Sponsors of events should bear the following points in mind:

1. They, or their designees, should assure that safety regulations are in place and are provided to participants.
2. Safety officers appropriate to each service branch should be appointed.
3. Participants and their officers need to be made aware of the event safety regulations.
4. Drills and inspections need to occur according to the event standards.
5. Enforcement of the standards must be universal and must include the exclusion of non-compliant individuals and/or units.
6. Adequate medical support personnel must be on-site.

To sponsor an event and ignore these principles is to court disaster. Such a cavalier attitude opens the doorway to litigation and places human beings at risk. Injuries such as those experienced by Rod Bulley have happened to others, but such events are extremely rare. This rarity will make any future such accidents prone to litigation as they need never occur. Yet, the safety standards commonly used at events are still not universally applied. In this writer's opinion, it would be better if the few events that have a lax attitude toward safety disappeared rather than risking the injury of even one more person.

CONCLUSION

Accidents happen and nothing and nobody is perfect. When mistakes come they come in various degrees of seriousness. In some instances mistakes are a minor matter. In other cases, the level of potential damage encapsulated in a mistake makes it far more destructive. The use of any sort of weapon falls into this latter category of extreme risk. Through the use of proven safety procedures, the inherent risks of using and handling Civil War vintage weaponry, inclusive of artillery pieces, can be managed. With the neglect of these safety building blocks—the possibility of catastrophe increases.

By maintaining safety as a preeminent element at any reenactment, regardless of size, living historians behave in a reasonable manner. By taking these reasonable approaches reenactors reduce the likelihood of a repeat performance of what sadly happened at the *Gettysburg Train Raid* in 1997. It would not take too many legal settlements to provide a serious disincentive to any group considering the hosting of a reenactment of any sorts. Let the reenacting community take charge of these circumstances by demanding that core safety practices become part and parcel of all events. If an event is marked as one that allows poor practices to go unchecked leave it and spread the word that others should do so as well. Demand high levels of drill and safety awareness in your unit. Practice a "safety first" approach at every event you attend. The costs of ignoring the lessons of history are too obvious and painful.

- Chapter 8 -

LEADERSHIP: THE GUN SERGEANT
&
HIS CREW

Artillery played a major role in the Civil War. Cannoneers at battles such as Malvern Hill, Stone's River, Gettysburg, and countless other engagements exerted a tremendous impact on the outcome of events. Gunners sighted in on towns such as Petersburg, Atlanta, Vicksburg, and Fredericksburg and created previously unheard of damage to American cities. All in all, artillerists contributed a tremendous amount of energy, ingenuity, and effort to the events of the Civil War.

Gunners generally had a higher degree of training than was given to infantry or cavalry troops, and in many ways artillery was the most professional of the service branches. Under sometimes galling fire, commanders and crews were expected to perform their duties inclusive of serving the guns precisely, maintaining their rate of fire, and defending their position. While casualties in the artillery were much lower than in the infantry there were fields where many gunners were stricken. At Gettysburg, for example, Union General Henry Hunt estimated that one third of his cannoneers in the center of the Federal line on the third day were reassigned infantrymen, because of casualties among the gunners. On the march, artillerists often had to manhandle their guns over bad roads or no roads at all. Wherever they moved, gunners had to care for the approximately 100 horses in a battery.

Portraying and commanding these men, and appreciating their performance on the reenacting field, demands some knowledge of the role artillery played, and the role the men play within the batteries. Artillerists served bravely throughout the war. Their story is somewhat neglected and that is unfortunate. When thinking about artillerymen and their roles it is best to first consider the basic building block of that branch of service—the battery.

UNIT STRUCTURE

The basic unit of artillery was the battery. On the Federal side, a battery typically consisted of six guns. Confederate batteries often had four guns. There were ofttimes few consistencies among the guns of a Rebel battery, which could include rifles and smooth bores, Parrotts and Napoleons, etc. The result of this mix-and-match approach was increased complexity in the logistics of handling and supplying the batteries. Federal gunners typically did not face this logistical nightmare but it sometimes did occur.

The battery commander, usually a captain, had overall responsibility, but each gun crew was under the command of a gun sergeant. Because each crew operated independently as it served its gun, the commander had to depend on the skill of his sergeants to ensure the effective operation of a battery. The sergeant had to see that his men as well as their equipment were in constant readiness. This NCO was responsible for the machine-like precision required of his crew.

Today, in reenacting batteries, it is reasonable to expect that unit officers, including gun sergeants, should take a leadership role in researching their battery. People filling such leadership roles should find whatever unit histories that are available on your company, as well as histories on the theaters and battles in which it took part. To be a true leader and a contributing living historian, become informed about what happened to the battery whose insignia you wear. For those not participating as a reenactor, the study of individual and unit histories deepens your grasp of what life was like for artillerymen in the Civil War.

UNDERSTANDING ORDNANCE

The most common full-scale guns used at reenactments today are bronze Napoleons, 3-inch ordnance rifles, and smaller Parrotts. Although many other types can also be found on occasion, these workhorse pieces reflect the backbone not only of reenacting armies but actual Civil War batteries. The crew and officers manning these guns need to be aware of their characteristics and ammunition and whether they are manning an original or a reproduction piece.

The bronze 12-Pounder Napoleon became the workhorse fieldpiece of the Federal Army in the late 1850's and was widely used by both sides in every theater of the Civil War. It was capable of sending a 12-pound solid shot from its 4.62-inch bore more than 1,700 yards with a 2.5-pound powder charge. The Napoleon could be used with lethal effect on infantry when canister rounds containing twenty-seven 1.5-inch balls were unleashed with shotgun-like efficiency. At reenactments, a blank charge of about one pound is typically used with the powder encased in aluminum foil.

The Napoleon is a heavy gun, with barrel and carriage weighing about a ton. This can make it a chore to move by hand. In the 1860's teams of horses ridden by drivers seated upon the three left side horses of a six-horse team maneuvered these pieces under harsh enemy fire and over rough terrain. Guns were manhandled into position and were moved back on line after each discharge. On occasion, guns were prolonged via ropes in retreat or advance. On the road, the Napoleon could be a bear to move through mud and other natural impediments. In modern reenactments, where horses are rare, it is the gunners who must provide the sweat and muscle to get the guns where they need to be.

The 3-inch ordnance rifle was considered by contemporaries to be the superior full-scale rifled gun. The rifled barrel allowed it to fire a shell or case shot more than 1,850 yards with a one-pound powder charge, and with much greater accuracy than a Napoleon. The 3" ordnance rifle was used effectively against infantry by firing shrapnel shells with short fuses. The ordnance rifle is considerably lighter than a Napoleon and can more easily be moved to and on a battlefield.

The 10 and 20-Pounder Parrotts, with 2.9 and 3.67-inch bores, respectively, were also rifled guns used by both sides during the war. Although not as widely used as the 3-inch ordnance rifle, Parrotts could fire a variety of ammunition, including case, shells, canister, and a form of solid shot known as a bolt. Canister fire was generally ineffective due to the scattering effect the rifling produced that in turn widened the spread of the rounds too much to create the impact of a Napoleon firing the same projectile. Ten-Pounder Parrotts can be seen at many reenactments, although more usual in the East than the Midwest and the South. Twenty-Pounder Parrotts are rare and represent the outer edge of manageable size for reenacting.

During the Civil War, artillery typically fired three or four types of ammunition. Solid shot of varying sizes was used in counter-battery fire, against fortifications, or at longer ranges against massed infantry. Case shot was a fused, thin-walled projectile filled with balls, which exploded before contact. This usually was used against infantry. Shells were fired with pre-cut fuses, designed to detonate on or before contact and produce shrapnel. Canister was a can filled with several dozen iron balls packed in sawdust. Loaded in single, double, or triple loads, canister was the most feared anti-personnel round available to an artillery crew against infantry at 400 yards or less.

Obviously, only one type of ammunition is used at a reenactment - a blank round. These range in size from three ounces to around one pound. Bigger guns such as Napoleons require larger charges to produce a realistic effect. A smaller gun such as a three-inch ordnance rifle requires a much less substantial charge. Preparing the charges is the responsibility of the sergeant and is a prime safety factor given the destructive potential of black powder. A comparable responsibility in the 1860's would be the gun sergeant making sure that ordnance in the limber and caisson for his assigned gun were well stocked and maintained.

Blank rounds are rolled by forming a cylinder of aluminum foil with one end closed. The appropriate powder charge is poured in and the top is carefully folded shut and tamped. The rolled rounds are then locked in the limber chest until the time comes to fire them. Carrying out this simple process properly is crucial. A leaking round rammed into the bore of a cannon that still has sparks or coals could result in a premature firing and serious injury. Of course, rolling rounds should only occur in a secured area away from any combustibles. Spectators need to be cleared away when this procedure is undertaken

DRILLING THE CREW

A gun sergeant is responsible for a one-ton weapon firing a charge equivalent to a
volley from an infantry battalion. Drill is an essential component of safety in handling this weapon, but a balanced approach is called for. An approach to drill that leaves no room for fun can lead to demoralization. To be so laid back that drill is sloppy is dangerous and unbecoming. A balance must be struck which combines efficiency, safety, and fun. This requires a gun sergeant who knows what he is doing and how to work with people. As in the 1860's the gun

sergeant is primarily responsible for the efficiency and interchangeableness of the men on his gun.

When drilling, the sergeant must watch for safety infractions such as sponging or ramming too far ahead of the bore or coming to the ready in an unsafe position. He must impress upon his crew their responsibility for handling the gun in a safe manner. Every round that is fired has the potential for disaster. The gun sergeant must be constantly vigilant as the piece is manned, cleared, loaded, fired, and shut down.

There were variations in artillery drill as practiced in the Eastern and Western Theaters, both during the Civil War and among reenactors today. The different drills all are based on the same principles, however. Members of the crew have a numbered position, with consistent duties assigned to them. These specific duties can change depending on the protocols being followed by the battery, but the needs of the gun are similar. The piece must be cleared with the worm, sponged both wet and dry, and ammunition loaded, rammed and prepared for firing. The gun then must be primed and fired.

The two forward gunners stationed to the right and left of the muzzle, do the bulk of the physical labor. The Number 1 man is charged with wet sponging and ramming while the Number 2 cannoneer worms and loads. The Number 3 man thumbing the vent has a very real responsibility for the safety of the entire crew, at a reenactment as well as in real combat. The Number 4 man with the lanyard must pay close attention to the sergeant in firing and is responsible for setting the friction primer and ultimately discharging the gun. The men working the limber (Numbers 5-7) must be careful about when the ammunition chest is opened and how charges are handled.

Although the roles of each of these positions can vary between batteries, it is important that the responsibilities be clearly spelled out and understood by each member of the crew. Therefore, it is essential that the battery be consistent in the drill being used. It is confusing and dangerous when each gun sergeant within a battery handles the drill in a different way.

Although it is tempting to place selected men in certain positions because of their experience and it makes sense in combat to have the most experienced men in the key positions at the vent and muzzle, it is a good idea to rotate crew members during drill. In the Civil War era all men on a gun had to be adept at each position. Battlefield attrition necessitated flexibility of use among artillerists. Then, as now, it is important to assure that each artilleryman familiar with the requirement of each position. The sergeant must be sure that each crewmember feels comfortable in his assigned position. If mistakes occur, a cannon firing a blank round can become a massive safety hazard. As was the case in the 1860's it is still a vital fact that the gun sergeant must ingrain in each crewmember an understanding of the stakes involved every time the gun is fired.

Drill is also a good opportunity for living history. Spectators enjoy watching a crew handling a gun, and narration from a knowledgeable crewmember can make the drill a learning experience for the visitors as well as the crew. Drill in the Civil War built camaraderie and teamwork. In our own age it can be an educational tool for the participants and spectators alike.

While drill is important, it can also be tedious--so know when to quit. Reenactors do not enjoy drill much more than soldiers did during the war. There is a difference between being well drilled and being drilled into the ground. If drill becomes too prolonged or ritualized, members will lose interest and performance will drop. As the reenacting season progresses and members become adept in the drill, reduce the time spent on it. However, always spend time with new members to assure their proficiency at the drill and do not put them in critical positions too early. Gun sergeants during the war were faced with training new men even at moments of battle's high tide. Never place an inexperienced or uncomfortable person in a position of responsibility on a cannon.

MAINTAINING EQUIPMENT

Artillerists were responsible during the war not only for maintaining their guns but also all the related equipment and horses. While there are some mounted artillery groups at reenactments, horses are missing from most batteries today. So, this area of coping with the numerous horses needed to complete a battery is a chore most living historians portraying artillerymen will never face.

If the equipment used by a crew is substandard, safety and performance problems can arise. This writer remembers observing a gun sergeant at a national event trying to explain to an officer why there was loose powder in the limber chest and why a steel priming wire capable of sparking was being used to prick the charge. It is the job of the gun sergeant to see that these embarrassments do not occur.

It is a good idea to put together a comprehensive checklist of all items that must be in place prior to any battle reenactment or firing. These include friction primers, gunner's haversack, rolled and secured rounds, primer pouch, priming wire and sling, full sponge bucket, two rammers, pliers, gimbal, gloves, ear plugs, thumbstall, worm, sight and plumb.

Having all items present, in their proper place, and in good working order is a matter of safety as well as convenience. It is the sergeant's job to see to all of these logistical and safety matters. A checklist will help to avoid the problem of discovering something is missing after having taken the field. The gun sergeant is responsible now as in the past for the proper operation of all equipment associated with the piece.

The worm should fit the barrel and be honed enough to catch the foil residue left after a firing. Sponge heads should fit the barrel and be in good condition without rips or tears that could result in a part of the covering coming off in the barrel. The priming wire must be long enough to actually puncture the round. A way to assure this is to place the priming wire into the vent when the piece is unloaded and mark its face just above the vent. This gives the gunners a way to see that the priming wire has been fully inserted.

After a battle scenario, the gun sergeant should see that adequate attention is paid to cleaning and maintaining equipment. Sponges should be soaked and cleaned. Any damaged or defective equipment should be set aside for repair or replacement. All implements that came from the limber chest, including gloves, the gunner's haversack and thumbstall should be put back where they came from. It is the sergeant's job to see that what has been used has been restored to its proper place and state.

ASSURING SAFETY

Drill, maintenance, and a thorough knowledge of the equipment all contribute to the safety of the gun crew, other participants and spectators during a reenactment. But the gun sergeant also is responsible for routine precautions not specific to artillery.

Perhaps the easiest – and one of the most easily overlooked safety checks a gun sergeant should make--is for ear protection. A musket being fired can result in ringing of the ear or other damage to hearing. A cannon can deafen a person. Exposure to artillery fire without ear protection is foolish. Each crew should have earplugs in the limber chest, or in their personal possession, and the gun sergeant should make sure that every crewmember uses them. Civil War artillerists were deafened via their service. Modern day reenactors need not create a sensory disability due to their hobby.

Each crew must also have adequate water on the field. Even with all the other dangers faced, heat still is probably the most dangerous element at a reenactment. Having a full canteen can mean the difference between an enjoyable event and an emergency room visit. The gun sergeant, at inspection prior to the battle, should always check every participant's canteen. Actual Civil War gun sergeants were charged with overseeing the welfare of their platoon. So too are their modern day counterparts.

Each member of the gun crew and his commander should also be aware of health conditions that could limit his activities on the field, and the gun sergeant should keep an eye out for crewmembers that are pushing themselves too hard. The gun sergeant has a very real responsibility as a safety inspector and voice of reason to maintain a safe reenacting environment.

CONCLUSION

In the Civil War the backbone of an artillery battery was the gun sergeant cadre. These firm soldiers needed to know both the operation and maintenance of their equipment and the psychology of the men. The spirit needed to create an effective fighting force was primarily a product of training and leadership. Soldiers in the 1860's became comrades through the daily grind of soldiering. The clash of battle cemented their unusual and shared experiences. Effective gun sergeants created the spirit of comradeship needed to make a unit a cohesive force through the way they handled the individual members of their group. A well-trained and motivational gun sergeant served as a leader for the members of his crew. Through his leadership that gun crew became a team that could effectively replicate its drill field perfection under fire. Each crewmember was willing to sacrifice everything to support their teammates. Such an amazing suppression of the individual's basic instinct for survival is primarily a result of the unit cohesion spawned by gun sergeants. Therefore, in looking at an artillery battery, the true human rocks of the unit's foundation were, and are, the NCO's filling the difficult role of—gun sergeant.

- Chapter 9 -

ROLES & RESPONSIBILITIES WITHIN AN ARTILLERY BATTERY

A field artillery battery was a society unto itself. With over one hundred men and dozens of horses as well as a mountain of equipment & ordnance, a field battery was also a complicated logistical challenge. During the Civil War artillerists on both sides served in batteries that bore great similarities to one another. Even though the war divided Americans in a lethal way the experiences of artillerists on opposing sides bore great resemblances to one another. In order to understand the "artillery experience" it is important to grasp the different roles and responsibilities that were encompassed with the unit known as a battery. What follows is a synopsis of the basic and differing responsibilities that cannoneers fulfilled within their respective units. It truly mattered little if the individual artillerist served in Battery B, 4th US or the Washington Light Artillery—these duties were virtually the same. Modern students of Civil War artillery and potential artillery living historians alike would do well to understand these duties.
In addition, by knowing something about the various duties fulfilled by Civil War artillerists a living historian deepens their impression while also having a better grasp of both history and safety on the field of reenacting battle.

CAPTAIN: The battery commander, the captain was responsible for the training, service, and effectiveness of the unit's men and equipment. The captain was in charge of fulfilling the recruitment role aimed at assuring an adequate supply of men to fill the various roles within the battery. Captains also were in charge of soliciting replacement horses from artillery higher ups and other sources inclusive of civilian impressments. Depending upon the army's organization an artillery captain reported to an artillery battalion commander, a division Chief of Artillery, or an infantry brigade commander. This chain of command varied according to time, circumstance, and varying army organizations. The captain commanding a six-gun battery, as was the norm in Federal service, was in charge of as many as 170 men and approximately 100 horses. A four-gun battery, which was more typical in Confederate service, with four horse teams had a minimum of 71 men and 45 horses to achieve effective trim. Promotion from the captaincy was slow and limited as the injury and mortality rates among artillery officers was much lower than in the infantry.

FIRST & SECOND LIEUTENTANT: Each of these officers had responsibility for a discrete section of the battery. Overseeing a platoon of cannoneers and their equipment a section chief was responsible for upwards of 40 men and 20-30 horses plus gear. The lieutenants received their orders from the captain. Section chiefs were charged with maintaining an appropriate inventory of their men's gear, uniforms, and accoutrements. They were called upon to requisition necessary replacement equipment including ordnance, uniforms, leather goods, and shelter. On occasion a section would be ordered out on picket along with a cadre of infantrymen. Such duty afforded a section chief an opportunity to gain field experience, conduct an independent command, and show their mettle. On the march lieutenants were often assigned duties such as bridge building, overseeing fording operations, and traffic control. While marching, section commanders rode abreast of their cadre and worked to lessen straggling. In battle, lieutenants directed the fire of their sections from either horseback or on foot. Upon the absence of the captain the senior lieutenant took command of the battery. In cases when such a promotion was permanent an attendant increase in rank generally did not occur. Promotion for lieutenants was a glacial process.

SECOND LIEUTENANT (Chief of the line of Caissons): The most junior officer in the unit this man was responsible for the oversight of the battery's caissons and attendant ordnance. The caisson chief had the corporals assigned to caissons, drivers, and any extra men assigned to him. When not engaged with the enemy, this officer often served as the captain's adjutant. In battle, the chief of caissons was charged with keeping the ordnance out of the line of the enemy's fire but near enough to the battery to assure ease of replenishment.

FIRST SERGEANT: The ranking NCO in the battery, the First Sergeant reported directly to the battery commander. The first sergeant was responsible for administrative duty, assignment of the men's duties, fatigue duty, roll calls, and daily reports. The ranking unit NCO also worked to develop the picket rotation, posting guards, stable call, horse grooming, and equipment repair. This man was responsible for the training of other NCOs in their duties. During battle, the first sergeant had no assigned responsibility but stayed near the captain and fulfilled whatever role that officer established for him. In case of emergency the first sergeant could be moved to chief of the caissons thereby freeing another officer for section command. In dire emergency, the first sergeant did assume the command of a section.

QUATERMASTER SERGEANT: Under the tutelage of the captain or first sergeant the quartermaster sergeant was responsible drawing clothing, personal gear, rations, and small arms for the men. In addition, the quartermaster was responsible for all details of the teamsters and their cartage. Drawing replacement gear often involved traveling with the wagons to a depot that could be days away. In battle the quartermaster sergeant had no specific combat responsibilities. Generally, the quartermaster remained with the wagons or fulfilled other duties assigned by the battery commander.

GUN SERGEANTS – CHIEFS OF THE PIECE: The gun sergeant was directly responsible for the men, horses, and equipment connected to his gun. Generally this arrangement included one cannon, 9-13 horses, the attached caisson/limber, and the entire gun crew. All men involved in the gun sergeant's crew were to be cross-trained and capable of filling any role on the gum. In battle, the gun sergeant dismounted and generally assumed a position to the rear of the piece. In action the gun sergeant was to assure that the section chief's orders were heard and carried out by the crew. The sergeant was to closely observe the effectiveness, aim, and direction of the gun's fire. Gun sergeants were to pay particular attention to both the performance of the gunner and the status of ordnance. When necessary the gun sergeant called for the bringing up from the caissons of replenishing ordnance. If horses were killed or wounded and had to be removed from harness the gun sergeant made sure that appropriate actions were taken. On the march, the gun sergeant rode beside the left lead horse and served as a platoon guide. Gun sergeants were ranked in order of seniority and were referred to as Second, Third, Fourth Sergeant, etc.

CORPORALS – GUNNERS: The gun corporal was directly responsible for the men and equipment of a gun detachment. This responsibility included seeing to the daily needs of the men assigned to the gun and limber.

Additionally, the gunner needed to keep a sharp eye on the status of all equipment on the gun, limber, and men serving the piece. On the road the gunner marched near the piece and worked with the men to maintain marching order. In combat the gunner carried out the gun sergeant's orders and aimed & sighted the piece. Firing orders were relayed to the gunner who gave them to the crew. Sighting the piece was fairly complex due to recoil and often took more time than the actual loading procedure of a well-drilled crew. Corporals were rated by seniority with senior members serving as gunners and juniors working as chief of the caissons.

CORPORALS – CHIFS OF THE CAISSON: The primary job for these NCOs was the care and maintenance of the limbers and caissons. A chief responsibility was making sure that each limber chest was replenished with ordnance and ready for combat. Corporals had limited responsibility for drivers who typically responded to the orders of the lieutenant serving as Chief of the line of Caissons or the gun sergeants. When marching the caisson corporals were generally on foot near their caissons. Under combat conditions the caisson corporal made sure his platoon's ordnance was secure and ready for disbursement to the forward limber as needed.

PRIVATES – CANNONEERS: Each of these artillerists was trained in the fulfillment of an assigned position. They were also trained so as to be adept at all other gun positions as well as the role of driver. The cannoneers received their orders from the gun sergeant serving as chief of the piece. On the road they marched near their gun and frequently were called upon to lend their muscle to its movement. Fords, mud, snow, swamps, and steep grades all offered severe challenges to the horses and men assigned to the gun. In extreme emergencies, when speed was of the essence, the cannoneers were ordered by the battery commander to link arms and ride on the limber and caisson chests. This mode of transportation was rare as it seriously depleted the horses. As of 1862 general orders in the Federal artillery service called for the men to march with their pieces.

PRIVATES – DRIVERS: These enlisted men served as the riders and stewards of the horses used to move guns and ordnance. Each driver was responsible for a two-horse team as well as their harness and equipment. The drivers rode on the left horse and were charged with the watering, feeding and grooming of the team. These men were generally selected because of their experience with draft animals but that was not always the case. Under fire the drivers were responsible for successfully bringing the gun, limber, and caisson of their assigned piece into the correct position. This dangerous task also involved calming horses, tending to wounded animals, and unharnessing or removing dead or severely wounded horses from position. Once the line of guns was established the drivers were involved in observing for any necessity to relocate. In combat drivers tended to their animals and watched for enemy rounds that overshot the primary targets and descended upon the rear echelon troops. Drivers assigned to supply wagons or the traveling forge were usually farther in the rear with reserve forces.

PRIVATES – TEAMSTERS & WAGONEERS: Serving under the direction of the quartermaster sergeant these men saw to the movement and care of the supply wagons, forage carts, traveling forge, and sometimes an attached ambulance. These men generally received a slightly higher pay rate akin to a corporal's salary. An interesting responsibility was guarding the forage from marauders from other allied units. Each wagon generally was drawn by two to four mules whose harness and equipment had to be tended to. On the march these men and their wagons were at the rear of the column and sometimes to the rear of the entire army with the reserve train. Normally, a battery would have four to eight men detailed to these positions. Sometimes these posts were filled on a rotating basis but that was not the norm. In other instances the wagon drivers were assigned to the brigade quartermaster and removed from battery command. These drivers were sometimes seen as shirkers who stayed away from the fighting. However, they fulfilled an important and necessary logistical service for the battery.

PRIVATES – ARTIFICER & FARRIER: Specialists, these men were craftsmen who had unique and vital talents. The artificer served as a blacksmith responsible for repairing and making necessary metalwork and tools. The farrier was involved in assuring that the many horses and mules were properly shod. This was a very arduous task considering the number of animals that were encompassed within a battery. While some batteries assigned more than two men to these roles that was not the norm.

PRIVATES – EXTRA MEN: Most batteries maintained a relief corps of extra men who were used as replacements for men wounded, killed, sick, or on leave. These men were dilled on all gun positions and as drivers. They served in various roles and worked on an as needed basis. These extra men marched and stayed during battle with the section's caissons. They were assigned by the first sergeant to fulfill a variety of duties also on an as needed basis. The role of being an extra man was a temporary one as attrition took its toll within a battery. Bear in mind that although battlefield casualties were much lower in artillery units than in the infantry sickness was as common. Since disease was the true grim reaper of the Civil War, men serving in batteries often fell prey to microbes rather than bullets, shot, or shells. Extra men filled those vacancies until they too fell victim to some illness or injury.

PRIVATES – MUSICIANS: A battery was allowed up to three musicians by regulations. However, generally this number was limited to one or two buglers. The bugler or buglers were assigned to the captain's staff and were mounted. They kept close to battery headquarters and relayed numerous calls to the unit. Calls such as 'In Battery', 'Commence Firing', 'Cease Firing', and others were used in combat. Other more mundane calls such as 'Boots & Saddles' started the troops day off with a bang. When not fulfilling these duties buglers were often used as clerks serving the battery commander.

PRIVATES – GUIDON: Serving in a role similar to an infantry color bearer the guidon bearer was also on the captain's staff. In an age when dust, fog, and black powder smoke could mask the battlefield the guidon bearer filled a necessary role of recognition. Serving as a unit guide the guidon bearer's position in battle evolved to become approximately 20 yards to the rear of the central limber in the battery. The mounted guidon bearer was selected by the captain based upon courage, trustworthiness, and dependability. In camp the guidon bearer was responsible for the appropriate casing and storage of the colors. As was the case in infantry regiments, a battery's guidon was as a banner that represented the espirit de corps of the men. It was to be defended to the death by its bearer.

PRIVATES – GUARD MOUNT: Artillery units posted guards in a manner similar to but at a reduced amount as compared to infantry battalions. Pickets were posted with a minimum of two guards on duty at all times. Generally one guard was posted to oversee the unit's ordnance, guns, limbers, and caissons and protect them from unwanted guests. Another guard was posted with the battery horses to protect them and their forage. This post was less favored as it involved calming spooked animals and untangling harnesses.

CONCLUSION

Each of the jobs encompassed within a battery's structure had a purpose and meaning. On days when the roads were a sea of mud and each yard was a nightmare of suffering, the men in a battery must have questioned why they ever became an artilleryman. In battle, the need to stand by their pieces while enemy batteries concentrated their fire upon them must have tested their mettle to the maximum. Horses could be a seeming instrument of the devil when they spooked, tangled their harnesses, and then resisted any restoration of the status quo. However, artillery batteries generally became well-oiled military machines. In fact, an argument could be made that within the Union armies no branch of service demonstrated so consistent a level of excellence and proficiency as the artillery. One need only think of the consistently proud service rendered by Federal artillerists at places such as Malvern Hill, Stone's River, Gettysburg, Antietam, and Spotsylvania to realize the veracity of this perspective.

With a high degree of discipline and proficiency, artillerymen on both sides consistently rose to the challenges of war. While Confederate cannoneers generally were dogged by fewer and less reliable supplies & ordnance they too rose to the occasion when called upon to do so. These men, blue and gray, served well throughout the war and filled a fascinating role within their respective armies. Their contribution is best understood when the functioning of the elemental unit of artillery structure is investigated. That unit was the battery, its equipment, animals, and men. Each such battery a microcosm of artillery functioning as well as a sort of military family for the men who served within it. We honor their memory by better understanding what work they did and how they endured it.

Sources

Dean S. Thomas, *Canons: An Introduction to Civil War Artillery,* Gettysburg, PA:
  Thomas Publications, 1995.

Greg M. Romaneck, *Civil War Artillery for Enthusiasts & Reenactors,* DeKalb, IL:
  Marliese Press, 2002.

http://www.cwartillery.org/aguns.html

http://www.cwartillery.org/hansen.html

– Chapter 10 –

Civil War Reenacting at a Time of Real War

"How many that are now happy and full of life, looking forward with confidence to the laurels that may be won, before the struggle is over will be silent forever in death! or, worse, perhaps lamed and maimed for life!" In this way did Mary Webster Loughborough describe her view of war just prior to an anticipated engagement at Corinth, Mississippi in 1862. While that battle did not indeed come off, Mrs. Loughborough, who was the wife of a Confederate officer in General Pemberton's army at Vicksburg, eventually saw the reality of war play out in a manner she once had so aptly predicted. For those of us who attempt to recreate the lives of Civil War soldiers and civilians it is essential to realize that those folks actually lived through a cataclysmic war that rended the nation. During the war's course lives were lost or unutterably changed as a result of the fighting.

Now, we live in a complex time when American service men and women are in harm's way across several theaters of operation. At a time when actual warfare is taking place some thought should be given to the overall appropriateness of "recreating" a war that claimed so many lives. In a time of war the hobby of reenacting Civil War events can be egregiously misunderstood and misrepresented. Reenactors, themselves, can be party to this misreading of living history if they simply go about their habitual business without thinking about the world around them. At its most basic such thought should address a couple central questions—"Should I be reenacting warfare when real bullets, shells, and bombs are killing or maiming

Americans and other nationals? Is what I am doing on the reenactment battlefield prudent and ethical when other folks are really fighting a war?"

What follows are ten questions that might be wise to consider in a climate that is so different than just four years ago. If you believe that people look at reenactors in exactly the same way they did prior to the wars in Iraq, Afghanistan, and upon global terror cells then you may well be naïve. Therefore, take a look at these ten points and accept or reject them as you may. But, do not mindlessly go onto the reenacting field in this day and age without giving some thought to the issues contained in this short piece.

1. **Am I maintaining an accurate demeanor during reenactment battles?** It has always looked odd to me to see Union and Confederate "soldiers" laughing in the ranks while supposed death and carnage was taking place all around them. Those parties who like to take a hit and then sit up to take pictures certainly alter the way in which the viewing public will perceive a sham battle. In this era when some people attending or participating in an event may have a personal stake in the ongoing wars that are taking place out there, it is thoughtless the act in a childish manner during a reenacted combat situation. If your unit is near enough for the crowd to see and hear you then you should attempt to recreate a Civil War soldier and not someone who is "playing soldiers" as they might have in childhood. Take the moment seriously enough to put on a good show and, thereby, commemorate the suffering and fear that the lads of '61-'65 must have felt.
2. **Are you mixing your personal political beliefs with 19th century history?** One of the great things about living history is that you are afforded an opportunity to interact with the public. People will come up to

you and ask things about your clothing, weaponry, accoutrements, and Civil War persona. If you interject your egotistical political beliefs into the conversation, even in a veiled way, you both dull the mirror of living history and act in a pedantic manner. What if your self-appointed need to compare the current squabbles about Confederate battle flag displays with Civil War history does little more than irritate or inflame the public? What is the point of that act anyway? What possible connection could a controversial 21st century issue have to do in the life of a supposed 19th century soldier or civilian? People who come to reenactments to spectate or participate did not come to hear your political outpourings. Muzzle them and save them for more appropriate venues.

3. **Do you foment division in your unit by your free flowing and wagging modernist tongue?** Over the past few years some very sad events have occurred in both American and world history. Just as during the Civil War, innocent lives have been lost for reasons that do not always appear crystal clear. Are you helping to built unit cohesion and comradeship by bringing up current events subjects among other reenactors that are open to vigorous debate? The seeds of disunion can be sown via thoughtlessness or boorishness in any social group. Reenacting units are no exception to that proviso. Try to be part of the ties that bind your unit together and not the solvent that washes them away.

4. **Do you argue with spectators if they disagree with your viewpoint?** At a time when there is a great deal of debate over certain governmental actions in our own age does it really benefit anyone to engage in such debate during your recreational time? Further, is a Civil War reenactment the place where

arguments regarding contemporary issues should occur? I think not and when they do it can result in an undermining of the entire pretense of an event. When you come to a living history or full-scale reenactment try to have a good time. If you cannot enjoy yourself in your passionate hobby in an age when war, violence, terrorism, and economic uncertainties exist where can you? Try as best you can to think about friendships, safety, Civil War social history, and the things that you enjoy at a reenactment and not points of disagreement about current events.

5. **Do you recall that the actual Civil War was a tragic series of events and not just the source of your hobby?** It is all too easy to roll around in the grass, pretend to be wounded, and then hop up to go off to the vendors for an elephant ear or crab cakes. The war claimed more than 630,000 lives. It severed lifelong relationships in a bloody way. Families were left bereft and grieving. Yes, the Civil War also represented factors such as courage, sacrifice, bravery, and comradeship but at what cost? For some reenactors playing with black powder or understanding the most arcane element of drill or stitchery appears to be more important than grasping even a modicum of the lives of those 19th century Americans. People, the Civil War was a terrible crucifixion of the nation and not just the source of an interesting, albeit quirky, hobby. Keep that in mind while also remembering that other young people in different American uniforms are at this very moment paying similar costs to those borne by the men in blue & gray and their long gone families.

6. **Have you reflected on the appropriateness of participation in public battle reenactments while actual battles go on?** The decision to reenact or not

is a personal one. Whatever choice a person makes in this regard, so long as it is based upon reflection and thought, is a good one. But, to fail to even consider that there might be something untoward about pretending to kill and be killed when an actual war is going on is sophomoric. Whatever conclusion you come to should be based upon some thoughtful consideration. If, after such reflection, you feel you can go onto the reenacting field of battle—then do so. If not, but you would like to participate in this hobby in some other realms—great. If you cannot stomach shooting at people while the nightly news talks about combat losses—so be it. Just think about what you are doing and why.

7. **Are you taking greater care to know your audience at school presentations?** Imagine beginning a school presentation wherein you naturally stress the death, devastation, and human costs of the Civil War. Just as you begin to describe some of the medical practices used in the 1860's a student begins to cry. Unbeknownst to you, her cousin has been wounded in the Middle East. Where do you go from there? If you are going to talk about war with children you and their teachers had better know these sorts of details before you commence. There is too much suffering going on during a war to make things worse by unintentionally pouring salt in another person's wounds. Ask the school staff if any of the students you will be interacting with has suffered any recent losses or has friends or family overseas. Then use that information to influence what you say and how you say it when you present.

8. **Are you prepared to handle criticism for "playing soldier?"** Even though you may have the most educationally based and altruistic reasons for portraying a Civil War soldier some folks are not

going to understand your need to don a uniform at a time when they feel unjust or costly real wars are being fought. Some families with children in the armed services will be proud of the heritage saving activities that reenactors engage in. Others will look askance at people who would "play war" while people's lives are being destroyed overseas. You may well get criticism at parades, dedications, living histories, and larger events. How will; you handle it? It is best to think that scenario through before an angry, adamant, or bereaved person confronts you. Only you can construct the ultimate correct answer to the handling of such a situation for yourself. But, showing patience, listened rather than arguing, expressing condolences, or restating what a person is saying without arguing the merit of their case are ways to defuse such rhetoric. Remember, you are not obligated to argue with people during your recreation hours. However, once you set foot on the reenacting field you are a performer with responsibilities to your public. Be prepared to deal with criticism and it will be far less onerous once it happens.

9. **Have you carefully considered your event selection or is it done out of habit?**
Perhaps these are not the years to go to the annual shoot-em-up powder burn at Smallville, USA. Take a second look at the places you go as a reenactor. Do you think the way certain events you are familiar with do a respectful job of showcasing the life of Civil War Americans? Or, on the other hand, are they really farbfests that are somewhat embarrassing to you? If the later is the case then do not go. Media specialists who can justly point to the Smallville type events and chortle at the superficiality of this hobby have taken too many potshots at the reenacting community. This type of embarrassment can

transform into indignation if grown men and women are seen as mimicking mankind's most destructive event—war—at a time when the real stuff is costing people's blood and futures.

10. **Have you considered the question—"Am I a living historian or just an overgrown child playing in the yard?** A living historian is generally a person who has studied an era, some key aspects of it, the social history of a stratum of society, or the persona of individuals in a given moment in history. A reenactor is a person who attempts to recreate some aspect of history. The two terms can be inclusive or exclusive depending upon the broadness of an individual's scope and their competency. Neither a living historian nor a serious reenactor is interested in solely "playing soldier." I think it would be disingenuous to believe that some aspect of interest in the soldier's experience did not enter into a person's reasons for being a military reenactor. However, if all you are interested in is dressing up in your woolies and burning powder every weekend during the reenacting season then you are not either of the two categories noted above. In such instances you really will have a difficult time explaining to some person who lost a loved one to death in war why you are doing what you do on the reenacting "battlefield."

Reenacting has been a part of my life since 1992. Over those years I have been more and less involved in the hobby. For the past two years issues of familial loss, work stress, and conflicting family interests all took me away from much of the hobby. Beyond those barriers I must admit that the factor of warfare in the Middle East colored my willingness to go out and act out things that, in our own era, troubled me deeply. Now, I have returned to reenacting and see it as an avenue for education, camaraderie, sharing, and respect to those who fought the Civil War. But that attitude took a while for me to come by. Hopefully you can at least give some thought to this wonderful hobby and why or why not it retains its decency for you in the times we live in.

– Chapter 11 –

Sleeping Without a Tent: Tips to the Troops

"We marched back to Corinth in a cold, drizzly rain, and as I didn't have my blankets, I was wet through. I suffered that night as we had only green wood to make a fire. It stopped raining so I got my clothes partly dried. I lay on the wet ground to sleep, but would get so cold that I would have to get up and hover over the smoky fire. I put in about the most disagreeable night of my life, and was nearly sick when I got back to camp." Thus did Private Elisha Stockwell, Jr. of Company I, 14th Wisconsin Volunteer Infantry describe one terrible, but predictable, night in his Civil War military career. In Private Stockwell reenactors can take heed of his uncomfortable example and apply those lessons to their own efforts at campaigning.

The ability to recreate the life of a Civil War soldier with reasonable accuracy is one of the primary draws in reenacting. One way in which a reenactor can recapture the essence of a Civil War soldier's life is to attempt to sleep in the field without a tent. While such a Spartan sleeping arrangement is fraught with difficulties and may not be everyone's permanent cup of tea, it is a fact of life that many troops during the war were forced to experience just such a sleeping scenario. Therefore, why not at least occasionally consider leaving the canvas tentage behind and spending a night under the stars?

What follows is a very concise outline of steps a reenactor can take to spend a night, or a weekend, out in the field without a tent. While this writer in no way wishes to infer that such campaign camping should be the standard operating procedure for troops in the field, it is possible that such an arrangement may help create some amazing reenacting memories. On a personal level, while I have not always slept without a tent I have done so at several national level reenactments. I can still remember lying awake in the evening, listening to the sounds of camp and looking up at the night sky after a long and memorable day in the field at places like the 135th Chickamauga. I also recall spending several nights at a major Gettysburg reenactment in different sleeping locations with nothing but the sky and my ingenuity to keep me dry in changing weather circumstances. Those memories remain with me and are to a large extent the product of how I chose to pack and sleep over the weekend. The choices we make in terms of material goods and arrangements will help shape the memories we have of events, places, and actions not only in reenacting but also in other aspects of life.   In order to better prepare for sleeping *sans* tent a reenactor should consider the following points and use them in an advisory manner.

Level off the Ground

Elemental though it may seem, the first task of a campaigner is the carefully check out the ground they have chosen to sleep on. If you are careless in following through in this first step you may well find yourself unable to sleep well due to roots, rocks, and detritus that will inevitably find soft spots in your back or ribs to torment you. Take a few minutes to prepare the ground upon which you will repine and you will consider yourself a lucky campaigner later on.

Establish a Moisture Barrier

In campaigning, as in any hiking/camping exercise, an essential element is to block moisture from below. By first placing a gum blanket or poncho on the ground a campaigner creates a moisture barrier that will serve several important purposes. First, this foundation layer will help keep the sleeper dry in times of rainy weather. Once the ground becomes even modestly saturated moisture will wick up into the sleeper from below. Therefore, by lying on a relatively leak proof surface, the campaigner is provided a first line of defense against a soaking from the ground. This is also true in humid weather when the "dews & damps" of the field will drench you unless there is a barrier to their progression. Finally, in colder, fall weather the moisture barrier transforms into an insulation source that will help regulate your body temperature and act as a dam against cooling from below.

Create a Sleeping Pad

In backpacking, most hikers of any distance carry with them a lightweight sleeping pad that helps their tired bones recuperate in the night. Of course, reenactors do not have the luxury of carrying such a half-pound item with them. Yet, they can use their imagination to create some sort of padding to lie on after a hard day in the field. At many events straw is provided and that can be used to form a padding beneath the would be sleeper. In other instances downed pine branches may be scrounged from the woods and they can serve in a similar vein. If no such conveniences are available the campaigner can carry a second wool blanket or a shelter half to lie on above the ground cloth or poncho moisture barrier. In this is the arrangement the campaigner is doubling their ground insulation and providing themself with at least a slim layer of padding to aid in the pursuit of sleep.

Layering is Good

If you are trying to experience the romantic elements of sleeping out under the stars your heart may be in the right place but you must be practical as well as idealistic. Weather changes and the forces of nature are remorselessly unpredictable. The clear evening you lay down in can become a cold and wet night. Therefore, consider the value of layering. Any experienced mother or father knows that dressing children in layers during cold weather is the preferred practice. Likewise, outdoorsmen & women generally use a layering approach to deal with the potential ravages of falling temperatures or precipitation. Thus, when campaigning, it is wise to adopt a similar approach. After establishing your moisture barrier and padding, begin the process of layering. If weather is chilly use your shelter half, a second blanket, your great coat, or other external clothing items to create a series of layers above you. The layering pyramid will create insulation levels that act together to trap body heat and keep you warmer than you might expect. Remember that the combined insulation effect of your layers will be far greater than their individual value. Also, bear in mind that your body sheds heat from its extremities. Keep your hands, feet, and, in particularly nasty weather, your head tucked into your layers. In this turtle-like manner you will feel warmer and cozier.

Make Sure to Have a Waterproof Topping

Your final and top most layer needs to be a waterproof one. You never know when weather will change and it is best to expect ill fortune on this front. Therefore, use a poncho or gum blanket to establish a tarp effect under which you have a reasonable chance of remaining acceptably dry. When packing for an event consider the value of carrying two ponchos or a combination of a poncho and a gum blanket. Civil War veteran's faced with the ordeal of the march & camp often made such a choice. You can only carry so much weight and every ounce you select should have value to you in the field. The extra pound or so that a second poncho represents may be a wonderful investment of energy as it could save a weekend that otherwise might have been rained out. When you are sleeping and a few drops fall but leave you alone because you have established a rain resistant top and bottom layer to your camp—then you will appreciate having two rain proof items available.

Create a Pillow

From an orthopedic standpoint sleeping without a pillow is a surefire way to experience back, neck, or general pain. In the field a reenactor should strongly consider creating a pillow in as realistic a fashion as possible. In your possession are items such as a backpack, haversack, well-corked canteen, and clothing bundle that can serve in this role. When you turn in have an arrangement made where you will have some head and neck support. I have found that any or all of the aforementioned accoutrements can ably serve as a pillow. You will sleep better and feel more revived in the morning if you follow though and gerrymander some sort of pillow.

Shed Wet Clothing

Hypothermia is a danger that exists and dogs backpackers, hikers, and reenactors living in the field. The temperature does not need to be abysmally cold for the ravaging effects of hypothermia to take hold. Wind and wetness are contributing factors in hypothermia cases. Therefore, if you have spent the day in the field on a drizzly, cold, and windswept day you need to get out of your wet clothing and warm up. One way of doing so is to shed your gear and wrap yourself up in the layers you have established for your bedroom. Drink warm liquids and bundle up so that your own inner furnace can recharge and replenish you. If your shivering and cognitive disorientation persists the time has come to pack it in and seek out either help or new living conditions. Beware the numbing and potentially deadly effects of hypothermia in the field. Officers & NCO's need to be well versed in the symptoms of hypothermia and closely observe their troops when conditions warrant.

Have a Back Up Plan

Imagine yourself heading out to an event with the noble idea of campaign camping in your mind. Once at the event, you realize that the drenching or numbing weather conditions make your high-minded concept seem more like a sodden nightmare. There is no shame in changing a bad plan. Have a back up idea in mind. Carry a shelter half and decide when or if you need to seek out canvas protection. Feel no shame in crawling into a comrade's tent to avoid the event destroying effects of a soaking. Scrounge around, like Civil War soldiers did, and locate alternate sleeping arrangements in case of inclement weather. I recall going to a national event out east and having to scrounge sleeping locales on each of the three nights of the reenactment. Due to rain on two nights I found a battery wagon and an unsuspecting officer's tent fly to curl up under and sleep. I stayed dry and felt good about using my wits to avoid a bad situation. The artillerymen were welcoming and we talked about the ill effects of weather. The sleeping officer never knew I slept under his canvas and he did not need to know about my insubordination. At any rate, have a reserve plan and do not be ashamed to use it. As John Beatty of the 3rd Ohio Infantry wrote in his memoir, "Dash is handsome, genius glorious: but modest, old-fashioned, practical, everyday sense is the trump, after all, and the only thing one can securely rely upon for permanent success in any line, either civil or military."

Conclusion

While, at first blush, the idea of sleeping in the field without a tent may strike some reenactors as ill advised I would counter by saying that if we wish to recreate the life of Civil War soldiers we should make some sacrifices. In no way is this article intended to push an agenda of discomfort down the throats of readers. Conversely, all that is being suggested is that by occasionally spending a night under the night's sky a reenactor can create a living history memory that will potentially deepen the experience of an event. Leander Stillwell of the 61st Illinois Infantry Regiment once wrote, "I think that a man who has never spent some wakeful hours in the night, by himself, out in the woods, has simply missed one of the most interesting parts of life."

If you are up for it, plan accordingly, carry the right gear, and have a back up plan in mind you too can experience the sensations described by Leander Stillwell. If, on the other hand, you plan badly or are betrayed by Mother Nature you can experience a night like Ira Blanchard of the 20th Illinois described in his memoirs, "Rain came on and continued through the afternoon and all night. We had no shelter, and to lie on the ground with the water underneath and the rain pouring down on us was not pleasant. I found a good corner of the fence, put two rails across, then stretched myself on the rails and covering myself with a rubber blanket, and said to myself, "let it rain, who cares," and in this position slept soundly all night."

In order to avoid the "sound night's sleep" of Ira Blanchard while also enjoying the experience of campaigning, a reenactor needs to think ahead. Perhaps the way to go is to pick an event a year to begin tent-less camping and then see if the shoe fits. At any rate, sleeping without a tent at a living history event, or in a wilderness setting, can be both accomplished and enjoyed. If you are interested in trying something new please consider the hints included in this piece and head out to field with an eye on the stars and no barriers between yourself and the world around you.

Sources

John Beatty. *The Citizen-Soldier: The Memoirs of a Civil War Volunteer.*
    Lincoln, NE: University of Nebraska Press, 1998, ISBN: 0-8032-6141-1

Ira Blanchard. *I Marched With Sherman: Civil War Memoirs of the 20th Illinois*
    Volunteer Infantry. Lincoln, NE: toExcel Publications. 2000,
    ISBN: 0-595-01200-0

Leander Stillwell, *The Story of a Common Soldier.* Kansas City, MO:
    Franklin Hudson Press, 1920, ISBN: 0-8094-4034-8

Elisha Stockwell. *Private Elisha Stockwell, Jr. Sees the Civil War.* Norman, OK:
    University of Oklahoma Press, 1985, ISBN; 0-8061-1921-7

– Chapter 12 –

Ten Reasons To Be A Civil War Artilleryman

In many ways being an artilleryman in reenacting can be compared to the lot of the proverbial "stepchild". At many living histories, mid-sized reenactments, and larger regional or national events the artillery becomes a branch of service that is relegated to holding the chair while the more robust and omnipresent infantrymen sit at the table. Cannons are cumbersome objects and their movement on the reenacting battlefield is both rare and unwieldy. In many instances, infantrymen will fail to take seriously the impressions, dedication, and hard work that go into being an artilleryman. Yet, despite these elements of scoffing at artillerymen that sometimes arise being a cannoneer is an impression that has much to be said for it.

While it is true that there is a great deal of logistical hassle inherent in an artillery impression there are far more benefits than disadvantages. Being an artilleryman may not be the most numerous or glamorous impression but it can become a highly satisfying one.

In some ways, an artillery impression provides advantages absent from all other branches of service open to living historians. What follows is a brief summary of ten keynote reasons why the pursuit of an authentic artillery impression may be just the right thing for a current or potential reenactor.

1. **FAMILY ORIENTATION**: While it is not uniformly true there appears to be a general consensus among reenactors that artillery groups tend to be more open to a

family orientation. Many artillery units welcome spouses and children as part of the group. Attached civilian impressions are the norm with many artillery reenactment units. If having your family be a part of your hobby is important you are much more likely to be able to follow that dream in the artillery than in the somewhat more exclusive infantry.

2. **EMPHASIS ON TEAMWORK**: There is no doubt that infantrymen participating in events are required to have a high level of expertise in drill. Infantry units unable to perform basic school of the soldier and company/battalion drill quickly stand out in a negative way on the field. However, the teamwork involved in manning a cannon is much more life preserving than that engaged in by foot soldiers. A gun crew is a team with each person having not only their own assignment but a huge safety inspector element as well. A well-drilled crew acts almost as one. The repetition involved in clearing, loading, and firing a weapon of potential mass destruction breeds a strong sense of both teamwork and camaraderie.

3. **LIVING HISTORY OPPORTUNITIES**: At many events members of the public are drawn to the cannons as if to a magnet. An original twelve-pounder Napoleon stands out in its bronzed dignity as an object that needs to be described and examined. Thus, at many events simply standing by the guns affords a living historian ample opportunities to speak with the public. It seems more likely that an artillery reenactor with a bent for public discourse will have more chances to interact with spectators than the sometimes reclusive infantrymen.

4. **CENTER STAGE PRESENTATIONS**: At small to moderate sized events the artillery makes a greater impression on the public than the infantry does. Pay attention to the crowd's reaction the first time a cannon fires and you will note that it is more impressive than that

resulting from the scattered skirmish fire of a few dozen hardy infantrymen. The public will be at fairly close viewing range at the more moderately scaled events. Therefore, artillerymen will make a bigger show for them than their infantry cousins. If you think of a reenactment as a form of performance art than the gunners are on center stage with other branches as supporting actors.

5. **ARTILLERY IS ECONONOMICAL**: It is far less expensive to get started as an artilleryman than any other branch of service. Once you connect with a reputable, authentic, and safety conscious unit all you need to purchase is your basic uniform with minimal accoutrements. The cost of a musket alone basically surpasses the introductory costs of an artillery impression. Cavalrymen are far beyond the scope of cost required in the artillery as they have a veritable host of horseflesh expenses. Thus, if the initial investment necessary to get started in the hobby is a factor you had best strongly consider artillery.

6. **THERE IS A PROUD HERITAGE**: If you have read very much about the Civil War you will come to realize that the artillery was a far more professional branch of service than the infantry. In the Union forces the artillery cadre was marked by discipline more akin to the regulars than that implemented in the volunteer infantry regiments. Southern units such as The Washington Artillery were highly polished and well drilled. In many ways, the Federal artillery stands out as one of, if not the most, consistently excellent group of men to serve on either side. One would be hard-pressed to find many instances when Union gunners failed to perform at an outstanding level in any battle. Being an artilleryman on either side represents following in the footsteps of men who not only served their country but also did so with an unusually high level of excellence.

7. **ORIGINAL PIECES**: In many instances reenactment groups have successfully restored original tubes on reproduction carriages and thereby brought historical artifacts back to life. Serving on an original gun is a thrill unmatched by many other experiences in reenacting. To fire a piece that was used at Shiloh, Atlanta, or Vicksburg represents a direct connection with our Civil War ancestors. Being able to tell spectators that the cannon they are looking at, touching, and observing was actually used in the Civil War is a wonderful living history treat. If you are fortunate enough to serve on such a gun take pride in yourself and the men who worked that piece in the 1860's.

8. **LONGEVITY**: Even though there are some physical demands involved in moving a cannon it is generally true that a person can survive in an artillery unit longer than in an infantry group. The energy needed to march, fight, carry a pack, and generally fight as an infantryman is far beyond what is normally required of an artillery reenactor. It can be very tough to move a gun on a hot and humid day or to manhandle it through the mud. However, those experiences are not the norm. If you are at a point in your reenacting career where you feel the energy reserves you possess are ebbing perhaps artillery is the ticket. If you are considering joining a living history group for the first time and you are fearful of the physical demands involved in infantry you probably stand a greater likelihood of having a longer reenacting career in artillery.

9. **COMRADESHIP**: The togetherness of a well-drilled gun crew is pronounced. Likewise, many artillery groups are marked by a tremendous sense of comradeship and mutual responsibility. Artillery groups are confronted by logistical demands that their less encumbered infantry relations avoid. At the end of an event an infantryman can reasonably walk off the field

carrying all he needs on his back and in his hands. It is impossible for an artillery battery to exit the field in this way. In order to function in any reasonable fashion an artillery unit must be built around a shared work ethic. Moving the guns off and back on to the unit's transport vehicles requires effort and teamwork. Coping with the seemingly inevitable deluges that congregate at many events pushes an artillery unit to pull together to even exit the premises. Out of this mutual dependence a much tighter sense of comradeship develops than is often observable in the more independently minded infantry groups.

10. **IT IS SIMPLY FUN**: Whatever impression you choose to develop, living history is a wonderful hobby. You will make friends, see historic places, and come to understand a small part of the original Civil War soldier's experience in a way that no book can convey. Although all impressions offer unique elements they can also become somewhat repetitive. If you can swing it try to "cross train" and have the ability to pursue two or more impressions. Consider making one of those impressions an artilleryman. Being on the field or in camp with a tightly bonded and well-drilled artillery unit affords a unique type of reenacting fun. Think about sleeping under an original gun on a battlefield such as Perryville, Prairie Grove, or Resaca in a way similar to that of our Civil War predecessors and you will conjure up the possibilities inherent in being an artilleryman.

In closing, please bear in mind that personal preferences in reenacting will vary. In
no way should an endorsement of an artillery impression be confused with belittling other branches of service. In a world where tolerance is not always in evidence it would be helpful to realize that there may well be "different strokes for

different folks". Within the range of Civil War living history impressions other reenactors sometimes deride artillery. Yet, the next time you glance at the guns on the field stop and think about how much effort it took to get those fieldpieces where they are. Then ponder the safety issues inherent in firing a charge of up to one pound of powder per round. Consider the dedication of people who transport an artifact weighing a ton, or more, across hundreds of miles and then see if your own commitment to the hobby is more profound. Being an artilleryman demonstrates a love of Civil War history not much different than that of other committed living historians. This is an impression worthy of respect and interest. It is also one that offers great possibilities to either new recruits or veterans seeking a change of pace.

– Chapter 13 –

Commonly Used Civil War Language

Living historians who are serious about presenting themselves in a manner befitting their nineteenth century predecessors should pause for a moment and reflect upon what qualities truly mark their impression as "authentic." While, on the one hand those material elements of uniforms, weapons, drill, and physical demeanor all stand out as obvious ways that a serious minded reenactor can work toward a high quality impression there are other, more subtle elements that are essential. One of these more inconspicuous parts of a skillful impression is language. If a reenactor is serious about presenting him or herself as a believable recreation of those men and women who lived through the Civil War then some attention to correct language is a must.

In using period appropriate terms, words, and phrases a reenactor can contribute to the global way in which not only they individually affect the people around them but also how an event in total is perceived. Have you ever stood in ranks, sat by the fire, or waited for drill only to have modern discussions break into your reverie and disrupt the flow of an event? Certainly, we live in the twenty-first century and only the most puritanical of living historians would attempt and/or expect no modern intrusions into the language of an event. Yet, if you are equipped with a vocabulary that at least roughly corresponds to that of a Civil War era American, then you can contribute to the overall authenticity of any event you attend.

By focusing upon the vocabulary commonly used by Civil War vintage Americans, a competent living historian can flesh out yet another part of a bygone age. It is all too easy to forget that language is an almost living factor in day-to-day life. Words and phrases that are unknown to one generation become commonplace within the next. By taking some time to learn a portion of the lexicon of mid-nineteenth century America reenactors arm themselves with a basic quality inherent in the lives of the people they portray. Further, a knowledge of vocabulary common to the Civil War time period can be helpful when reading primary sources or attempting to craft an appropriate first-person impression.

In order to better understand the value and purpose of mid-nineteenth century speech what follows is a small sampling of commonly used terms & descriptors from the Civil War era. A quick perusal of this sample may help the reader to understand how engaging and valuable language from those far off days may be to both them and their reenacting impression. In a very real sense the appropriate use of language stands out as one of the finest "how to" instructions that veteran reenactors can pass on to more neophyte participants. Thus, the terminology below is offered as a beginner's guide to discourse in a way that Civil War soldiers and civilians might both appreciate and understand.

A-1: Naval abbreviation used by insurance agents when determining the value of a ship. A letter denotation was used to classify the ship's hull. A number was used to rate the vessel's equipment.
Acknowledge the Corn, To: A generally southern phrase used to own up to a hoax or admit to a tease.
Autumn Divers: Organized gangs of thieves who lurked near recruitment centers in New York and other eastern cities where they robbed men of their bounty money.
Awkward Squad: Term used by veterans to describe the efforts of ill-drilled new recruits.

Beetle-Crunchers: Jocular term for the infantry.
Bog-Trotter: Slang term for those of Irish descent.
Boiled Rye: Derisive reference to southern efforts to develop coffee substitutes from sources such as parched rye.
Bully Soup: A hot cereal made from cornmeal and crushed hardtack that had been boiled. Sometimes mixed with ginger, water, or wine.
Busthead: Slang for a home-brewed alcoholic beverage.
Camp Canard: Gossip.
Carpet Soldier: A contemptuous term for state guard or militia soldiers who avoided front-line service.
Cheese Knife: Sarcastic term for an officer's saber or sword.
Chit: Fractional paper currency issued by sutlers and redeemable only by the person or unit to whom it was given.
Coffee Boiler: Term sometimes used to describe stragglers who were also referred to as *coffee coolers* or men who would only march after their coffee had cooled.
Comin' With A Bone In Her Teeth: Naval term used to describe a fast moving vessel marked by foaming water at the prow.
Crimp: Agents who got men drunk and then enlisted them in the army or navy.
Cross on Confederate Pontoons, to: A sarcastic Federal reference to wading a stream.
Dandyfunk: A nautical term for a stew made from hardtack, molasses, and salt pork.
Ditch Hunter: Term of disparagement for men who always ran for cover when fighting erupted.
Doughboy: A derisive term used by cavalrymen towards infantry.
Eat the Dishrag, to: To wipe your plate clean with your bread and then eat that too.
Embalmed Beef: Canned or "tinned" beef.
Fast Little Trick: Prostitute.
Flux: A generic term for the many diseases that led to chronic diarrhea.

Forty Dead Men: Soldier's reference to a full allotment of cartridges.
Forty-Rod: The worst possible whiskey—said to be lethal at forty rods.
Frumenty: A meal of wheat bran, milk, sugar, and fruit.
Gallinipper: Slang term for the common mosquito.
Give the vermin parole, to: To discard rather than kill lice.
Go in search of his rights, to: Sardonic term for a soldier who has fled the battlefield rather than fight.
Goober Grabber: Colloquial term for a Rebel soldier—often used in reference to troops from North Carolina or Georgia.
Gopher: Term for the common infantryman who often spent time in trenches or holes.
Go Up, to: To die in battle or hospital—to have your spirit ascend after death.
Green apple quickstep: Diarrhea brought on by an over consumption of green fruit.
Gump: A fool or a dolt.
Handcuffed Volunteers: Contemptuous term for bounty men who were prone to desertion and virtually worthless.
Hireling: Derogatory southern reference to immigrant troops who were believed to only be in uniform for a paycheck.
Hish and Hash: A meal of whatever edibles were on hand.
Hog and Hominy: A succinct reference to southern cooking.
Horse Collar: Term for a foot soldier's bedroll.
Hunt Gold, to: Term for a soldier's first combat experience—akin to "seeing the elephant."
Indifferent: An adjective used to describe inferior quality of either workmanship or a finished product.
Infernal Machine: Term for new weapons such as torpedoes or mines that were considering "Unsporting."
Keening: A word drawn from the practice of wailing at Irish funerals—sometimes used in reference to the yelling or cheering of men in battle.

Knucks: A band of New York City toughs who robbed soldiers and sailors after getting them drunk.
Latin Farmers: Term of reference for well educated German immigrants in the Union army who may have come to the US knowing Latin or Greek.
Leg Case: Slang for a deserter—a reference often used by President Lincoln in his correspondence and conversation.
Lincoln Coffee: A southern term for northern coffee that was yearned for due to shortages in the Confederacy.
Lobscouse: A stew made of hardtack, vegetables, and salted meat.
Lobster Backs: Slang for members of the US Marine Corps.
Lop-Ears: Slang term for German immigrant soldiers who may only have known a bit of English.
Louse Comb: Generally made of bone with closely spaced teeth this device was used to assist in delousing soldiers and civilians.
Men's Harness: A human harness to be used when mud or the steepness of terrain called for soldiers to hitch up and pull guns or wagons.
Mossyback: A man who evaded military service—a draft dodger who hid out in a swamp or similar refuge.
Mudscows: Slang for shoes and most specifically "Brogans."
Mudsills: Confederate slang for Union soldiers of common origin—also used to refer to working class people or "common folk."
Nationals: Confederate reference for Union soldiers.
Niddering: A synonym for cowardly or base—prevalent in the Cotton Belt states.
Old Bull: Derogative reference for salted meat.
Old Soldier's Disease: Also referred to as "soldier's disease" this term referenced addictive tendencies among veterans who had received an over dosage of morphine or opiates as painkillers when in military hospitals.
Open the Ball: Initiate battle.

Oysters: A Southern dish made of coarse cornmeal, eggs, and butter.
Panada: Another term for "bully soup" or a mixture of cornmeal, mashed hardtack, and flavorings—served as gruel.
Paper-Collar Soldiers: Garrison duty soldiers or those with a "Fancy Dan" appearance.
Passing Box: A name for white pine ammunition boxes.
Peas on a Trencher: Federal bugle call for breakfast.
Point Blank: A range at which bullets, shot, or shell travel in a straight line with no degradation in flight.
Possum Beer: A homemade brew of persimmons.
Puke: A Kansas term for a Southern sympathizer.
Pumpkin Rind: Union army term for a lieutenant due to their shoulder straps denoting rank.
Pumpkin Slinger: Nickname for smoothbore muskets such as the .69 caliber Model 1842 as well as many foreign imports.
Rag Out, to: Dressing in formal attire.
Robber's Row: Slang for sutler area.
Run: Small body of water usually a branch of a larger stream or a flowage smaller than a creek.
Sacred Dust: Reference to a corpse.
Salt Horse: Derisive term for salted meat.
Sauerkraut: Nickname for a German immigrant—sometimes shortened to "Kraut."
Scuttlebutt: A naval term used to describe gossip or camp rumors—derived from the name for a cask of fresh drinking water around which sailors gathered to talk.
Seed Tick Coffee: A substitute coffee made by Confederates that resembled ticks or insect larvae.
Semi-Yankee: Derogatory term used by Confederates to describe southern Unionists.
Sheep Dip: Term for inferior whiskey.
Skillygalee: A dish made from hardtack soaked in water and fried.

Skulker: A soldier notorious for avoiding combat and duties.
Slow Bear: Yankee slang for a pig.
Spare Wheel: Also referred to as a "fifth wheel" this term derived from the spare wheel carried on an artillery caisson but came to mean a useless figure.
Spotted Papers: Slang for playing cards.
Spread-Eagle Speech: Bombastic or unusually sentimental language.
Swallow the yellow dog, to: Derisive reference to southerners taking the Oath of Allegiance.
Toad Sticker: Slang for a bayonet, sword, or knife.
Tosspot: Slang for an alcoholic.
Turkey Driver: A Federal Provost Marshal.
Turnspit: A useless fellow.
Used Up: To be worn down—referred to units of troops or individuals.
Veal: A soldier or unit with no combat experience.
Wagon Dog: A soldier who feigns illness to drop out of ranks and try for a ride.
War Horse: A veteran of combat.
Web-Foot: A soldier without shoes.
Web-Footed Cavalry: Slang for infantry.
Wet Goods: Slang for alcohol.
White Glove Boys: A disdainful reference for eastern theater Federals coined by western Federals.
Wooden Overcoat: Barrel used to punish soldiers who were obligated to parade around camp wearing it.
Yellowback: Inexpensive paperback books marketed by sutlers.
Yuunk: An unpopular person—a term prevalent in correspondence from southern prisoners of war in particular those housed on Johnson's Island or Camp Chase.

Source
Garrison, Webb & Cheryl, *The Encyclopedia of Civil War Usage: An Illustrated Compendium of the Everyday Language of Soldiers and Civilians.* 2001, Cumberland House, Nashville, TN, $27.95, 274 pages. ISBN: 1-58182-186-7.

NOTE—Webb Garrison, a long-time contributor to the field of Civil War history and research, passed away as this, his final book, was being completed. His wife, Cheryl, completed this work with skill and purpose. That labor of love has provided Civil War enthusiasts with a valuable resource in their pursuit of a better and more authentic approach to recreating the time period they honor. Thank you to both of the Garrison's for their tireless pursuit of knowledge in this critical phase in America's history.

– Chapter 14 –

Living History's Place in A Time of Crisis

On September 11, 2001 terrible events took place in New York City, Washington D.C., and rural Pennsylvania. The terrorist attacks that claimed almost 7,000 lives will live on in the memory of Americans and others who were touched by them. What a terrible happening and one that remains virtually inexplicable in terms of scope and affect. In many ways those tragic events have changed the way in which Americans view themselves and their activities. People who once thought nothing of watching a violent movie or indulging themselves in leisure or travel now ponder on the appropriateness and relevance of those actions. In our own little corner of the world known as Civil War living history we too have been given cause for reflection on the hobby that we hold so dear. Is it relevant to dwell on the past when so much sadness resides in the present? Should I take part in a mock battle while people have real death so near to their hearts? Is what I do a glorification of war that was sanitized by our nation's seeming removal from real life violence so common in other parts of the world? Do I have the heart to go out in the field when all I feel is loss and sadness?

These and other questions have dogged me since the recent tragedies of September 11. In an effort to answer some of these questions I elected to participate with my father in a wonderful living history event held annually in Greenbush, Wisconsin. The Greenbush event has been hosted by the staff of the Wade House Historical Museum for approximately a decade. I have had the privilege of participating in this Civil War weekend a number of times and it is commonly rated as one of the premier Midwestern events. However, as I prepared to participate in the 2001 Civil War weekend I was troubled by the doubts contained in my aforementioned questions. I could not get past the feeling that donning my Federal uniform and hoisting my Enfield musket on my shoulder was somehow wrong at this time in our nation's history. I kept coming back to the feelings of heartbreak that the terrorist attacks had imbedded in my spirit. I doubted that many people would want to come out and see men and women recreating a time in American history where so much death was prevalent. Simply put, the feelings of value that I had imbedded in my ten years of Civil War reenacting were brought into fundamental doubt.

      However, despite my personal doubts I did carry through on my commitment to accompany my father on our trip north from Illinois to Greenbush. I went fully expecting to have uncomfortable feelings about my participation. I also went hoping the experience would be different than what I anticipated. Whatever the realities of attending my first reenactment since the September 11 disaster I was prepared to reflect on my feelings after and during the event. What follows is a brief summary of some thoughts and suggestions I came away from Greenbush with. That weekend was to become very meaningful for me. It taught me lessons about human nature that I will carry along with me for quite a while. Hopefully these humble suggestions will strike a chord of familiarity with readers who may well have recently undergone a similar thought process. These are lessons I will hold dear and I hope they ring true with you as well.

In Times of Grief We Need Friendship

Writers and practitioners far brighter than I can ever hope to be have chronicled the fact that most people who are grieving benefit from being with friends. The companionship of loved ones and comrades holds people together even in their darkest days. One need only think back to the experiences of Civil War soldiers, north and south, who lived through an age of death and devastation we cannot imagine. Yet, in so many of their letters what comes across is the way in which their connection with their friends in their unit helped them to get through. At Greenbush I was reminded of how valuable friends are. I saw comrades who I have stood in ranks with, looked after, and who have helped me. The feeling of belonging that being part of this wonderful hobby brings to us was reinforced for me as I marched, lay about, and simply hung around men and women who mean something to me. Participating in a living history event is very much an act of communion. We are part of a small group of dedicated individuals who strive to retain the memories of people who gave so much so that America could become what it is today. Coming together at our events allows that fraternity to continue. Thus, these living history weekends afford us a rare chance to be with people who understand our sometimes obsessive love of a certain historical epoch. In particular, at a moment in American history when so many previously held certainties are being questioned, it simply felt good to hang around camp or be in the field with people I value.

Living History Presentations Allow Us to Reeducate Young People About the Realities of War

The day before my trip to the Wade House event I had the opportunity to listen to a radio interview of a group of Massachusetts high school students. These youngsters discussed their views about possibly being called upon to join the armed services and fight for their country. What I heard over and over from these young people were statements like "It is honorable to die in war," "If I have to go it could be an adventure," "We have to fight to protect ourselves and I want to fight." Listening to these young people I was struck by how similar those words sounded to me. They harkened back to comparable renderings of young men in 1914 & 1861. At that time people went off to war with the conviction that it would be short, relatively bloodless, and glorious. Those Massachusetts teens made me shake my head and cry as I pondered upon how little we have learned about the realities of war and death. At Greenbush I was able to dedicate a significant amount of time to doing living history. In that context I was able to point out to groups of spectators, inclusive of adolescent and pre-adolescents, that the experiences of Civil War soldiers were not ones that they would really want to live through. War is hell and it cannot be refined. Despite the justness of any cause the horrible realities of war should be taught to our youth. Living history events create a wonderful forum for such peace education. By dedicating myself to that avenue of instruction I found Greenbush to help me replace the befuddlement I felt upon hearing those dedicated and misguided Massachusetts teenagers with a sense of positive action on my own part. In the wake of September 11 we need to stress to the public that we do not glorify war. We also would do well to remember both what the soldiers of 1861-65 fought for and what they went through..

When In Pain People Need to Be Able to Express Themselves

One thing I have learned over the past ten years is that it is often unwise to discuss modern political or social topics with fellow reenactors. All too often such discussions lead you to realize disagreements that you did not even know existed between yourself and your comrades. Further, such modern discussions can take you out of the 19th century moment that you are trying to create. Yet, at Wade House I was anxious to know what other people were thinking and feeling about current events. I must admit, I was fearful that what I would hear was hate tinged rhetoric solely aimed at achieving revenge regardless of the cost. Yet, what I actually experienced was an almost universal feeling of sadness and moderation. Virtually every person at that event who brought up the attacks felt some level of depression. They also hoped that justice would be done but not at the cost of other innocent lives either in the USA or overseas. I also found that being away from home and at a place that represented an activity they loved allowed people to feel better. Being out in the field on a beautiful Wisconsin fall weekend seemed to salve over the scars of the previous weeks. Thinking about the intricacies of drill allowed people to stop dwelling on the terrible TV images and ongoing media conjectures. Telling someone what they hoped would happen became an act of virtual prayer and contrition. I left Greenbush feeling better about humanity than I did when I was sitting at home watching CNN.

Seeing People Behave Compassionately Deepens Us

One thing that has always struck me about Civil War reenactors is that they will help one another. Time and again I have seen reenactors seize the moment and behave compassionately. If someone is overcome by heat people respond and help them. If a car gets stuck in the mud hands come forward to push you out. If you are lost and cannot find your unit somebody will take the time to assist you. Reenactors know that their hobby includes some elements of risk. They also realize that the people they portray lived at a time when helping their comrades was the order of the day. Such behavior stands in sharp contrast to the wanton acts of destruction that have dominated our psyches over the past few weeks. How many people have looked at those terrible images of planes flying into inhabited buildings and shaken their heads, cried, and wondered what kind of a species are we? Seeing people help one another aids the healing process and replaces these fundamental doubts with the knowledge that most people want to be decent. At Greenbush this basic truth in our living history community was reinforced. I saw veterans helping new recruits to learn the fundamentals of the hobby in a selfless and comradely manner. I observed people willingly providing others with gear, food, and shelter. I stood in line with men who I know would care for me if I was injured or overcome. This is not a novel living history experience but rather the norm. In this little recreational world we demonstrate event after event that people are essentially humane despite what sometimes happens. This is a reaffirming perspective and one that I am glad I was able to see.

Living History Events Give Us an Opportunity for Memorials

One thought that I had when I went to my first post-September 11 event was are we not behaving superficially at a time of great national tragedy? I wondered about the appropriateness of "playing soldier" when real soldiers are deploying for future battle.

These doubts plagued me and made me wonder if the time was right for such happenings. Fortunately, what I experienced at Greenbush eliminated those doubts from my mind. Yes, the battle reenactments were a part of the weekend. Yet, in my mind, and for many other participants, this was not an act of "playing war". Instead, it was a homage to men and women who 140 years ago set out on a terrible journey of four years. That journey helped shape the world we now live in. I did not sense a glorying in war or death. Indeed, as on no other reenacting field that I have set foot on, I sensed seriousness about what we were doing. At the conclusion of the battles a prayer and memorial activity was structured. Men clad in blue and gray stood in ranks with their respective colors fluttering in the gentle breeze. Thousands of common folk who came as spectators listened as soothing words of prayer for innocent victims were aired. Then, in an act of collective unity, Kate Smith's performance of *God Bless America* was played and we all were asked to sing along. I must admit that I was able to choke out only about half the words. Many other reenactors, spectators, and I found ourselves dabbing at our eyes and feeling a lump in our throats. Still, sharing that memorial moment helped me to realize that going to Greenbush was not only the right decision but also a necessary one. I had taken part in an activity that was in many ways therapeutic. Americans coming together to try to find solace in doing something they loved with people they respected. How could that be bad? It really cannot and it was not at the Wade House.

Conclusion

In camp at the end of the day our Federal battalion was asked to "rest on arms" and take a moment of silence in respect for those who died while we still live. While I stood there in my faded blue coat and tattered Hardee hat I thought about those poor people who lost their lives or who were maimed by a seemingly random act of violence. While standing there with my eyes closed I began to compose a slight revision to a poem I had written a few days earlier. As those words came to me I knew that our simple little hobby remains important to me and, hopefully, to others. What we do is not a vital act but it is a commemorative one. If we can recall what our predecessors sacrificed perhaps we can overcome the threats and tears that are so typical nowadays. I offer you the poem that came to me at Greenbush and hope that it will mean something to you. I am glad I went there and I will remember that event and its meaning for me for a long time.

September 11, 2001

Planes flown by angered men become bombs.
Tower-like buildings crafted for the ages burn and fall.
People leap to plummeting death – hand in hand.
Loved ones stand with tear stained faces holding pictures and wait for a miracle.
Missing people by the thousands each leaving a hole in the world.
How can we do these terrible things to one another?
What devils does the human spirit enfold?
We are beings who can create great beauty and wonder.
We are also able to be infinitely cruel to all life forms.
What can be learned from tragedies that shake our core?
Love is better than hate – kindness has nobility.
Violence begets violence – suffering affects us all.
The pain felt by a new widow or orphan in New York
is similar to that of their counterpart in Israel or Palestine.
Our lives are interconnected with those of people in far off lands.
Life is no longer as simple as it seemed to be.
We have much work to do in years to come.
Let us pray that this work yields peace and joy for the world's children.
We can learn from every experience – good or bad.
Even the seemingly unfathomable holds seeds for growth.
It is up to every one of us to reflect on these happenings and find some meaning.
In time there will be hope again, but now there is so much sadness, loss, and confusion.
We await hope's return with resolve but with tears in our eyes.

– Chapter 15 –

The Leave of Absence: One Option for Reenactors Who Feel "Played Out"

Every year veteran reenactors leave the hobby after dedicating time, energy, and money to it. At a time when the reenactor ranks are thinning in terms of participants it is interesting to think about why this process of dropping out occurs and options reenactors facing a termination of their pastime could consider. Over the past two years, after being an avid reenactor for over a decade, I began to feel that Civil War living history was becoming not only less important to me but also was changing into a barrier to other elements of my life. Thus, for the last two reenacting seasons I have seen my participation plummet and the reality of leaving the hobby I have loved for years looming before me. This change in my own thoughts and feelings about an activity that has not only given me many meaningful memories but also has allowed me to better understand the realities of the American Civil War is one that has led me to reflect upon where to go from here.

In the past two years I have changed from a person who once went to several national events a year as well as dozens of regional and local gatherings. How could such an alteration occur? What should I do next? Why have my feelings changed about an activity that once partially defined me? Hopefully, the suggestions that follow will be of some value to reenactors out there who also wonder if there is a place for them in future campaigning seasons.

To begin, a reenactor who feels the impetus to leave the hobby they have cherished should first pinpoint what factor or factors are driving their decision making apparatus.

For me, the diminishment of enthusiasm for reenacting had several key elements.

First, having done many events a redundancy began to set in. I would stand in the ranks and think, "Here I am again in Wauconda, Illinois and people are still childishly arguing about the results of the tactical." This element of sameness began to lead me to no longer go to many events because I had already "been there and done that."

A second factor that drew me away from events was the frequent bickering that seems to typify reenacting. The "political" element inherent in debates over authenticity standards, command structure, eastern versus western styles, and real-life political persuasions all decreased my desire to be around some people. This reality made it seem more profitable to simply stay away rather than spend a great deal of time and energy to go places where there was a possibility of having a bad time.

A third factor that set me up for a weaning of my reenacting commitment was the fact that my family did not typically participate in the hobby. Occasionally one of my children would grudgingly go along with me to an event or a film shoot but, by and large, I was the solo family member that had a love and interest in this activity. This solitariness, linked to the enormous time commitment that is inherent in reenacting, gradually drew me back toward more family-centered activities. I came to realize that it was preferable, for example, to skip reenacting in the summer and, instead, schedule backpacking trips or vacations with my family.

Another issue that moved me away from reenacting was that other interests grew while reenacting seemed to remain the same. Hobbies such as biking, hiking, or simply reading & writing became much more enjoyable than facing long car rides to do an activity over again that had seemingly already been done before. People do "move on" and change is inevitable.

Elements of my work also acted as a barrier to reenacting. Where once I could rationalize taking time off from work to go out to Gettysburg for a long weekend growth in the school district within which I labor made such hiatuses more difficult to arrange and justify. Also, certain work responsibilities made it unreasonable for me to be out of touch with my colleagues during the school year. Hence, a progression, good or bad as it may be, in my work responsibilities made reenacting at certain times of the year far less important or possible than it once was.

Finally, the dropping out of the hobby of some of my closest comrades left a void in the experience of being at an event. While there are still many reenactors whom I know and respect in the circles that I once traversed, some of my closest friends have come and gone. Their departure leaves a gap in the line of my sense of what I hope to gain at an event. I am no longer sure that the file closers of my mind and emotions can seal this gap.

Thus, facing these variables I began to stay away from the fields, camps, and forests that had once marked not only my experiences but oh so many hours of anticipation and recounting. I can still remember many amazing experiences that I would never have encountered if I had not been a reenactor. Standing in a mist shrouded Confederate cemetery near Resaca after a pre-dawn tactical at the 130th commemorative event still leaves me with chills. Watching the Rebel lines advance en masse at national events like Franklin or Gettysburg remains engrained in my memory. Standing in the ranks with friends who I would trust with my life on a blistering summer day while the red, white, and blue colors unfurled above us still rests in my soul. Yet, times change and life moves in different directions.

Based upon present realities and past experiences I am very tempted to simply walk away from reenacting and move on. In the past two years there have been a number of events I committed to go to and then backed out. In some cases, I had already loaded my gear into a vehicle and, when the moment came to depart, simply decided that it was not worth the effort. Still, I remain uncertain as to whether or not my current feelings about reenacting will remain and stay in place in the future. Thus, for myself and other reenactors who share some of this waning of the spirit, perhaps there is another alternative to grab a hold of rather than simply giving up on a hobby that once was their passion. Such an alternative is the concept of a leave of absence.

    Leaves of absence are somewhat common in a number of fields. For example, in education teachers or administrators occasionally ask for permission to take a yearlong leave to go back to school, raise a child, or pursue some other option with an eye toward returning to their district. In some cases, the person on leave never returns to the district that granted their request. Life has moved on in a direction that militates against a return and that person begins new endeavors. However, in most cases educators on leave do return. Once back, many educators find that their energy and enthusiasm have either increased or remained at a level necessary to accomplish a demanding and important job.

Why would reenactors who have dedicated so much time, money, and emotional energy to their hobby not consider simply taking a year off rather than ditching their beloved hobby? What follows are rationales for considering such a leave of absence prior to either returning to reenacting or reflectively deciding that it no longer suits you.

Reflect Rather Than React

    Decisions are best made after you think about alternatives. Rash decisions, sometimes based upon emotional rather than analytical reasons, can be poor ones. If you once loved taking care of your reenacting gear, planning the season's schedule, getting together with your pards, and being in the ranks try to take pause before you close that door forever. Take a year off and then see how much you miss or forget about reenacting. If, after time away from the hobby, you feel its pull again you can go back. If, on the other hand, after time away you realize that it has lost its relevance for you then move on.

It Once Had Value

If you have been reenacting for any length of time you must have valued the hobby in some deep way. No rational person would subject themselves to the heat, rain, dust, and weariness of reenacting unless there was a strong pull to participate. I can well remember the feeling of exhaustion after the 135th Chickamauga event. I was dripping wet, covered in dust, coughing from the dry campsites, and covered in spider bites. Yet, I was also exhilarated from campaigning over the weekend, being a flag bearer for my battalion, and having been part of an event full of comradeship and grandeur. Such memories count for a great deal. Although the bloom may be off the rose so to speak, reenacting once was very important to you. Hence, allow some time to pass before you divorce yourself from a relationship to a hobby and its members that once moved you.

Things Can Change

If your interest is waning and you take time to stay away from reenacting you may realize that your past participation pattern in the hobby does not have to be your future game plan. If, for example, you once went to twenty events in a season you may find that 3-5 events a year might be more advisable. However, if you are trapped by your past pattern of behavior you will burn out and no longer want to do any events. Your future pattern of reenacting may be radically different than what it once was. Take some time off and think about what level of participation, if any, you can still commit to Civil War reenacting. That level may be zero and then it is time to move on. If not, then ration your time in a way that allows you to meet not only your Civil War reenacting needs but those other competing ones that have contributed to your departure.

Look for Diversity

Most things in life do not have to be "all or nothing" experiences. In relationships, possessiveness can easily result in a breakdown of the bonds of affection. In the workplace, people who become workaholics are generally one dimensional and misguided. So too, in reenacting, those individuals who spend countless hours fixating on events, material issues, chat room debates, event planning, or all the other myriad elements of this hobby may well experience burn out. If you are at that point take some time off from the hobby and perhaps you will remember what elements of Civil War reenacting really are important to you. Maybe your niche is simply writing about Civil War history. Perhaps you should go back into the ranks and give up your position of leadership. Or, on the other hand, you may discover that all the time and effort once dedicated to reenacting is no longer relevant to you. Let some time pass and then think about novel elements of the hobby you can replug into and adjust to the future.

Material Objects Speak to Us

If you have ever stood in an exhibit and looked at material objects from the Civil War, or other time periods, you are looking at the physical manifestations of history. The sergeant's shell jacket that was once worn at Gettysburg and which you are now observing through a glass divider is the reality of what once was. So too are the elements of each of our impressions. If you are contemplating giving up the hobby you may be on the verge of selling off your gear. Stop—do not do this until some time has passed. Many times in the past I have been to events or unit meetings where a reenactor is selling off his stuff at greatly reduced prices. While this is a wonderful way for new recruits to get their kit together it always struck me as a sad moment. Each piece of your gear has had some meaning and personal history. When I look at my own equipment I remember certain past experiences. There is the bloodstain on my frock coat courtesy of the Antietam film production crew. The tear in my sack coat reminds me of thrashing through thorn bushes during the 130th Wilderness event in Virginia. The browned out look of my felt hat reminds me of the many hours spent on the march, drilling, or waiting for something to happen. My gear speaks to me of past events, weather, happenings, and people. Take a year off before you think about selling your stuff. Once it is gone the odds are quite steeply stacked against your ever returning. Also, some pieces of your uniform may have a special place in your heart and home even if you never return to the recreated field of battle. Keepsakes are OK even if the use they once had is but a memory.

True Friends Do Not Come and Go

If you stop and think about it one of the strongest pulls that reenacting exerts is that of friendship. If you do not feel connected to people in your unit, or the hobby in general, you will probably not remain in it. Comradeship was the cement that bound together units during the Civil War. Likewise, in the reenacting world, comradeship and friendship are the glue that allows people to cope with the many harsh demands that are inherently part of reenacting. I can still remember wedging into a company tent after the 135th Shiloh event was washed out. Looking around at my friends and comrades as water and steam poured off of each of us made a miserable situation seem relevant. I cared about those men in a way that allowed me to mildly understand why Civil War soldiers were willing to risk death in order to stand shoulder to shoulder with their comrades in arms. Friends are not always easy to make and the loss of friends is a tragedy. If your interest has dipped and you are stepping away from reenacting try to measure how much you miss those men and women who you used to cross paths with in obscure and famous bits of territory around the nation.

Political Realities Change

At this point in time I personally wonder if it is appropriate to recreate combat. We live in a time of terrorism, warfare, and uncertainty. Is it right to reenact terrible warfare at a time when American troops and civilians in a number of lands are dying in real wars? That is a political question that individuals can only answer for themselves. Yet, issues such as this one do influence people's decision to participate or not in Civil War events. Whatever the decision you make you may want to remember that political realities change. A war that might have seemed just at the outset may no longer fit that bill after certain truths previously hidden or misdirected come to light. So too can your own perceptions of your behavior. If now, due to political questions, you think it is inappropriate to don a uniform and recreate combat in some superficial way then do not do it. But, if in the future, your thinking shifts, reconsider what you should do and return to the hobby you once treasured.

In closing, my own journey as a reenactor has been wonderful. I have met people through reenacting that I will probably never forget. Because of various events I have visited places related to Civil War history that I probably would not have taken the time to journey to. Reenacting experiences have deepened my understanding of Civil War history and the life that soldiers and civilians lived in those dark days. I know what it feels like to sleep under the stars, heft a musket on a long dusty road, sleep in the rain, smell powder on a firing line, and cope with the demands of weather in the field. I have felt comradeship under harsh conditions and grown from it. I love the fact that I have done and seen what I have in my reenacting career. However, things change.

    In the face of these changes I will be considering a year off with time and energy once spent on reenacting being directed to other venues. In that time I will be thinking about my future role, if any, in the reenacting world. Hopefully, I will find a niche for myself next year and will continue on in a hobby that has meant so much to me. Perhaps the absence of reenacting will strike me before a year closes and I will know that a return to the field is necessary. However, if that is not the case, I will have taken the time needed to realize what I think and feel about this hobby.

  If you too are in the same place and are considering walking away from reenacting stop and take some time to give yourself a second chance. Thus, consider your time away from the hobby a leave of absence and not a permanent departure. You may wish to return and, if so, you will come back with a new purpose and plan. If not, then hold on to the many good memories that your experiences as a reenactor have given to you. Whatever road you choose, make the decision to travel it a thoughtful rather than impulsive one. Do not leave yourself second-guessing the steps you take or undervaluing the experiences you have had in the wonderful world of reenacting.

– Chapter 16 –

Taking a Hit: Ten Do's & Don'ts of a Forgotten Art

If you have reenacted for any length of time the following scenario will be all too familiar. Picture a sunny day with reenactors arrayed against one another on a flat field

As the "battle" commences the opposing sides confront one another in line formations or with skirmishers. The opposing sides fire at each other by company, file, and independently. The smoke billows across the field while a few hundred to a few thousand spectators watch. Minutes pass and the Union and Confederate troops continue to frantically load and fire. As the clash of arms progresses the spectators begin to comment on the fact that nobody is getting hurt. Time passes and, finally, one solitary soldier falls to the ground and remains lying dead on the spot. After a few more minutes a couple other soldiers drop to the ground—dead. Then, as the reenactment approaches its climax, a volley from one side destroys the opposition and victory is declared. The spectators leave somehow feeling that what they saw, while interesting, rings false.

Let's face it, in most cases reenactments are grossly unrealistic in terms of tactics and casualties. Reenactors who have traveled hundreds of miles tend to be hesitant to take a hit early on in most scenarios. When hits are taken they are almost universally either mortal wounds or immediate kills. Many reenactments feature very few casualties until one side or the other is devastated by the opposition's musketry or artillery fire. Folks, this approach is artificial, unrealistic, and poor theater.

What follows are ten simple thoughts or suggestions about taking hits during a battle reenactment. Some relate to safety while others are more geared toward authenticity standards. Hopefully, these humble thoughts will cause other reenactors to reflect on not only when, where, and why to take a hit but also the image that our actions on the field present to spectators.

1. **Take an Early Hit:** As noted above, it appears ridiculous to our public when men blast away at each other at unrealistically short ranges without any noticeable effect upon their foes. Casualties should occur throughout the course of a scenario and not simply near the end. There is no shame in being among the first to go down in a fight. If your unit is heavily engaged early in a scenario it is only fitting and proper for some of the men to take a hit in the initial stages of the fight. Remember, being an early casualty is both realistic and may save you the need to clean your musket afterwards. Seriously, a broader dispersal of casualties does offer a more meaningful and realistic image of Civil War combat to those people who have both taken the time to come out to the event and paid the admission fees.
2. **Take a Wound:** The vast majority of Civil War soldiers who were shot on the field of battle were wounded rather than killed outright. Conversely, on reenactment fields far more men are immediately killed in battle rather than being wounded. The public would be better served and educated if reenactors were more liable to portray a wounded soldier rather than a corpse. After you take your hit, fumble with your clothing and search out your wound. Countless accounts of Civil War soldiers who served in battle noted their wounded comrades pulling clothing open in an anxious attempt to see how badly

they were hurt. Follow suit and spend your time on the ground thinking about what it really would have been like to, in a state of shock, try to discover whether or not your life was ebbing away.

3. **Be aware of Your Surroundings:** Whenever you are planning on taking a hit be sure to keep certain safety factors in mind. Do not take a hit while your musket is loaded. The safety issues inherent in plunging to the ground with a loaded weapon appear self-evident but this happens at many events. Do not attempt a stuntman-like hit in order to impress everybody. People who do the grand hits eventually injure either themselves or reenactors around them. I still remember the large Federal infantryman who, at Cedar Rapids, Iowa, told me how "great" he was at taking hits. Later in the day, as I lay on the ground wounded, this big guy chose to come flying out of the ranks with a Sam Peckinpaugh-like hit. The would be stuntman, who weighed over 270 pounds, ended up stepping on my ankle, thigh, musket, and ear as he sprawled backwards. Avoid this type of theatrical and unsafe act. Also, if you are falling in front of a company, or reenacting in general, be sure that you have ear protection or you **will** suffer hearing loss. As a general rule, if you are going to take a hit be aware of where you are and what you are doing.

4. **Become a Walking Wounded:** In Civil War combat men were knocked out of ranks with a host of terrible wounds. For many of these lads, once the initial shock of being shot had settled in, the next step was to head back to the rear for some medical attention. Often, a comrade, due to compassion or fear, would assist the wounded man along the way. It would be far more realistic for reenactors to plan out their wounds in such a way that they become walking wounded who journey back in search of medical treatment. Having a pard help you along is also a realistic touch that will add an air of

authenticity to the field of reenacting battle. Once in the rear you have the option of participating in medical scenarios or, out of sight of the spectators, reconstituting and returning to the field of battle as a reinforcement.

5. **Do not behave In a Thoughtless Way on the Field:** Reenactments are not church services. The hobby, while important to its participants, is not a spiritual act to be taken so seriously that hushed tones and long faces must always be shown. However, a reenactment is a commemoration of the sacrifices that men and women made during the Civil War. Thus, if you are taking a hit during a battle reenactment you should attempt to present a realistic image to the public and the reenactors around you. It is crass to prop yourself up and watch the event. Popping a camera out of your haversack and becoming a twenty-first century photojournalist during a reenactment is inappropriate. So too are behaviors like smoking a cigarette, sunbathing, joking around accompanied with belly laughs, using your cell phone, or speaking with spectators. The bottom line here is, if you are portraying a soldier who is dead or wounded do so in a way that does justice both to the event and to the period we are portraying.

6. **Avoid Resurrection:** Yes, in smaller events it is difficult to have any sort of skirmish if troops are rendered permanently out of the scenario once they are hit. However, in such instances it might be better to avoid any sort of clash of arms save for picket firing because how believable is the scenario anyway? Nothing looks stranger on a reenactment field than to see soldiers alternately dropping and then rising up to "play" again. Some very fine events I have attended have a specific "No Resurrection" policy in their guidelines. If our goal is to present a teachable moment to the public in the form of a scenario then it is self-defeating to have people

popping back up on the field of battle after they have been hit.

7. **Avoid Extreme Reactions:** War is all hell and you cannot refine it. However, it is inappropriate to turn a reenactment into a crash course in the horrors of war. Try to avoid behaviors that will be so graphic that they will be offensive to the viewing public. For example, I once attended an event where a Union infantryman splattered fake blood on his face and went running into the spectators screaming "I'm blind! I'm blind!" In that case children, parents, and other viewers were frightened and appalled at the actions of this individual. Our role should be one of education and not shock. We cannot possibly recreate the suffering of war in any real way. We should thank God that such recreation is impossible as, although our impression should be grounded upon authenticity, do we really want to traumatize our public? Conversely, when every person taking a hit lies quietly on the ground we sanitize the realities of war. Wounded men writhed, murmured, called for loved ones, and ask for forgiveness. There is nothing wrong with acting like you are hurt when you take a hit. However, the extremes of blood and gore are best set aside for specific hospital scenarios where the public can choose or not to attend.

8. **Remain Aware of Your Surroundings:** Once you are down on the ground remember that the event is continuing around you. Troops may well march right over you. Horsemen might ride through the field. Artillery pieces may fire near you. Remain focused and aware of your surroundings. I recall once nearly being trampled at a small-scale event in Illinois by a cavalryman who was much more intent on firing his pistol than watching out for casualties on the field. Only a last minute lunge on my part kept me from being trampled by a large creature with a rider aboard him. Do

not lose sight of the scenario and possible incursions into your area.
9. **Stay in Character:** A casualty may have the greatest living history opportunities after the battle is over. Scenarios that include a medical component after the fight can afford some of the most memorable moments both for the participants and the viewing public. Events that include a gathering or inspection of the dead as a part of the event will leave observers with striking images that do justice to the losses incurred by our Civil War predecessors. By plays between comrades as one or more friends await medical attention allows for some creativity in a hobby that is often scripted and distant. Not everyone is comfortable with being a soldier experiencing an amputation or having your belongings rifled by enemy soldiers as you lie, dead, on the battlefield. Yet, what could be more realistic?
10. **Run Away:** Although not strictly a "hit" the sight of a soldier or soldiers breaking and running from the field is both memorable and very authentic. The American soldiers who fought in the Civil War were generally not professional fighting men. On seemingly countless occasions troops broke and ran from the front only to fight another day. This phenomenon struck not only green regiments but veteran formations as well. Running in the face of the enemy while yelling "We are sold out.", "I ain't gonna die!", or "We're flanked!" and discarding their gear presents a believable and impressive visual image. If planned out ahead of time such a scenario also allows officers an opportunity to react in a way that their real life Civil War counterparts would have. Remember that it was not only privates that fled from the enemy. The sight of an officer fleeing ahead of his men is one that would have occurred in battle and sets the stage for other living history opportunities back in camp or at subsequent events.

In closing, it is hoped that by using some of the suggestions above reenactors can help contribute to a much more realistic presentation at events. The public comes to Civil War events to learn and be entertained. It is our responsibility as reenactors to present an impression that is as meaningful and authentic as possible. Part of that process of informing the public is presenting a reasonably acceptable representation of Civil War combat. Combat means destruction, death, and wounds. Reenactors must take hits for a scenario to appear even mildly worthwhile. Timing, safety, and reaction are part and parcel of taking a hit in the right way. When scenarios feature such behavior they go much further in both capturing the interest of the public and doing justice to the people who really fought the war we recreate.

– Chapter 17 –

Illnesses of the Civil War Era: A Brief Compendium

On January 5, 1863, Emeline Ritner sat down to write to her husband, Jacob, who was far off at Vicksburg serving as a captain in the 25th Iowa Volunteer Infantry. While word had spread back home of some of the bloody repulses suffered by the Federal troops Emeline was more concerned with other matters, albeit ones that bespoke life and death matters, "You said I must go to Jefferson and stay two or three weeks. I should have gone two weeks ago, but couldn't get there at all. There has been no chance for some time and now I will not go, for the smallpox has spread so, that I know the people there wouldn't thank me for coming. I understand that they are very much frightened about it. I don't think I have been exposed to it at all, but I know they will be afraid to have me come right in the midst of it." (Larimer, p. 96)

Disease was a fact of life that shaped human behavior far more during the Civil War than it does now in the United States. In an age when medical technology had not progressed far enough to allow for protections we now take for granted, many diseases, once contracted, led to debilitation or death. In Emeline Ritner's case a vaccination procedure did exist against smallpox. However as Mrs. Ritner pointed out later in that same letter, even that was no guarantee of pure immunity, "Some have had it who were vaccinated and didn't go to bed. But I will tell you, it has spread from one end of town to the other." (Larimer, p. 96)

In order to more fully understand the thinking of 19th century people it is important to have a working knowledge of keynote social factors and language. Letters from that time period are often peppered with references to medical needs, nursing, home remedies, and doctor visits. At a time when almost 1.3 million Federal soldiers were treated for acute diarrhea and over 42% of Union troops were ultimately discharged due to chronic illness it is understandable that civilian discourse would focus so heavily upon disease. (Adams, p. 241).

What follows is a concise and dictionary-like compendium of commonly used medical terms of the Civil War era. While some terms are very standard in our own age, others are unfamiliar. It is hoped that this simple reference tool will afford some assistance in better understanding both the writings and thought patterns of our 19th century predecessors. This information has been primarily drawn from fascinating genealogical and medical websites that those readers wishing a more comprehensive look at this language issue should visit.

Ascendancy or Acescency: A tendency toward sourness of the stomach or slight acidity
Achor: A scalp eruption featuring great itchiness.
Ague: Common term for malaria
Apoplexy: Stroke resulting from a sudden stoppage of blood flow to the brain resulting in loss of movement, speech, muscle control or respiration.
Atavism: Term used to refer to hereditary traits or "breeding".
Barber's Itch or Rash: Infection of the hair follicles in the beard area thought to be transmitted by dirty shaving brushes – possibly impetigo.
Bilious Fever: General term for illnesses resulting in fever, vomiting, diarrhea, and oft times jaundice such as typhus, typhoid, or hepatitis.
Black Dog: Common term for depression.

Blackwater Fever: Severe form of ague in which blood was passed in the urine hence looking "black".
Bloody Flux: Dysentery.
Boneshaw: Sciatica or back pain.
Brain Fever: Severe and debilitating fever that was often mortal – possibly meningitis or Typhus.
Bricklayer's Itch: Eczema of the hands often resulting from skin exposure to mortar.
Bronchial Catarrh: Acute bronchitis with significant mucous discharge.
Camp Diarrhea: Typhoid fever.
Camp Fever: Typhus.
Caul: Birth membrane that protects infants in utero – thought to be a sign of good fortune if the infant was born with it still intact around the head.
Chilblain: Swelling with attendant itching and burning sensation of the extremities due to exposure to the cold.
Child Bed Fever: Infection in the mother following childbirth. High mortality rate and caused by unhygienic practices or examination.
Cholera: An acute and often fatal disease featuring profuse diarrhea, cramps, and vomiting. Caused by ingestion of contaminated water or food due to fecal matter contact.
Consumption: Tuberculosis or pulmonary tuberculosis and the associated wasting away of the body and spirit.
Corruption: Infection or degeneration of tissue.
Croup: Horse coughing associated with the swelling of the larynx, trachea, and bronchi in infants and young children.
Diphtheria: An acute infection of the throat, nose, and upper respiratory
 track – sometimes confused with scarlet fever and croup.
Dropsy: Fluid retention often due to heart or kidney disease.
Dropsy of the Brain: Encephalitis.
Dysentery: A number of disorders marked by intestinal inflammation and the evacuation of blood and pus.
Dyspepsia: Acid indigestion possibly chronic.

Efflux ion: Refers to "flowing out" but generally to bleeding
Emesis: Vomiting.
Empyema: A collection of pus in any body cavity but generally the pleural lining of the lungs.
Erysipelas: A contagious skin disease due to streptococcal infection of surface and subcutaneous tissues – often fatal due to corruption.
Excrescence: An unnatural or disfiguring skin growth or protrusion.
Falling Sickness: Epilepsy or seizure disorder.
Fatuity: Senility or dementia.
Fever & Ague: Common term for malaria.
Fit: Sudden attack of anything (e.g. coughing) – if unspecified a seizure.
Flux: An excessive flow or discharge of bodily secretion or excretions – often related to dysentery.
French Pox: Syphilis.
Furuncle: Boil.
Gallinipper: Common term for mosquitoes.
Galloping Consumption: Pulmonary tuberculosis.
Galloping Paralysis: Polio.
Gangrene: Death, decay, or necrosis of bodily tissue, usually in a limb, due to injury or disease resulting in a stoppage of blood supply to the affected region.
Gathering: A collection of pus.
General Yellow Jack: Common term for Yellow Fever.
Goiter: Enlargement of the thyroid gland resulting in moderate to severe neck swelling.
Gout: An inflammation of joints or extremities caused by dietary patterns resulting in a buildup of uric acid at the affected site.
Grip/Gripe/Grippe: Influenza.
Grocer's Itch: Skin disease caused by mites in sugar or flour bins.
Heart Dropsy: Heart disease.
Hydrophoby: Rabies.

Incubus: A night terror or illness that materializes or comes at night.
Infantile Paralysis: Poliomyelitis.
Intermittent Fever: Illness featuring periodic febrile patterns – probably malaria.
Itch: Scabies.
Jaundice: Yellowish discoloration of skin, whites of the eyes, and mucous membranes due to an increase of bile in the bloodstream.
Kinkcough or Kruchkusten: Common term for Pertusis or Whooping Cough.
Lockjaw: Tetanus.
Long Sickness: Tuberculosis.
Lumbago: Back pain.
Lung Fever: Tuberculosis or Pneumonia.
Lying In: Time of delivery of a baby – childbirth and labor.
Mad Hatter Disease: Psychosis often found in hatters who were exposed to large amounts of mercury used as part of the process of stiffening felt hats.
Malaria: A widespread and chronic disease caused by the bite of anopheles mosquitoes infected with parasites that then transfer to the human bloodstream. Periodic hatches of these parasites then result in the symptoms most significantly marked by high fever and chills.
Melancholia: Severe depression.
Miasma: Poisonous vapors thought to spread through the air and cause disease.
Milk Sickness: Poisoning resulting from drinking milk from cows that have consumed white snakeroot – often mortal it is best known for causing the death of Nancy Hanks Lincoln, President Lincoln's mother.
Mope-Eyed: Short sighted or blind in one eye.
Mortification: When used in a medical sense it refers to gangrene, necrosis, or severe infection.
Nervous or Nerve Fever: Typhus.

Palsy: Sometimes refers to stroke or, in other instances, some muscle paralysis.

Paroxysm: Usually refers to a convulsion or fit – anything that happens suddenly, violently, and unexpectedly.

Pulmonary Apoplexy: Severe coughing – possibly an asthma attack.

Quinsy or Quinsey: Pus-filled swelling of the tonsils that could be fatal due to fever, infection, or obstruction of the breathing passages.

Rag: As in "on the rag" – refers to menstruation.

Rickets: Disease of the skeletal system now known to be caused by a Vitamin D deficiency in childhood.

Scrumpox: Impetigo or severe skin rash.

Scurvy: Thought of as a seaman's disease it results in weakness, fatigue, spongy gums, tooth loss, and hemorrhages under the skin – caused by a lack of Vitamin C it was treated appropriately via fresh fruit and vegetable consumption.

Septicemia: Term used to refer to general blood poisoning.

Smallpox: Contagious viral disease featuring fever and blisters – vaccination was available with mixed results.

Suppuration: The production of pus – often seen as a precursor to healing.

Syphilis: Sexually transmitted or transmitted at birth via the mother to the newborn this disease featured a long and multi-staged emergence – incurable until the discovery of penicillin in 1928.

Tetanus: An infectious and often fatal disease resulting from bacterial intrusion of the body via wounds. Symptoms include severe muscle spasms, especially of the jaw, hence "Lockjaw". Transmission is now known to primarily result from exposure to bacteria in soil infected through horse or bovine feces.

The Drip: Gonorrhea.

Typhoid Fever: An infectious fever caused by ingesting food or water contaminated by sewage or contacted by

infected flies or a human carrier. Results in severe diarrhea and is frequently fatal.
Typhus: Communicable fever characterized by very high temperatures, headache, constipation, bronchitis, and a rash. Mouse or lice born this disease featured a high mortality rate.
Wet Nurse: A lactating woman employed to nurse another mother's infant.
Yellow Fever: An acute and often deadly infectious disease of warm climates transmitted by mosquitoes – also known as Yellow Jack, Yellow Jacket, & American Fever.

Sources

Adams, George Worthington, *Doctors In Blue*, LSU Press, Baton Rouge, LA, 1996.

Larimer, Charles F. (ed.), *Love and Valor: Intimate Civil War Letters Between Captain*
    Jacob and Emeline Ritner, Sigourney Press, Western Spring, IL, 2000.
http://www.paul_smith.doctors.org.uk/links.htm.

http://entomology.unl.edu/history_bug/civilwar/gallnippers.htm

- Chapter 18 -

SIMPLE REMEDIES OF THE CIVIL WAR ERA

It is a well known fact that medical practices of the mid 19th century, as compared to those of our own age, were indeed primitive. Along with the prescriptions of the physicians of that time period there were numerous common or "folk" remedies that were widely used. These remedies sometimes were passed from mother to child and became part of family medical practices. In more literate families the purchase of an almanac or housewife's guidebook often provided some compilation of generally accepted home interventions for common illnesses. What follows is a brief summation of some of these prototypical home remedies. These homilies are drawn from a fascinating little book entitled *The American Frugal Housewife*.

Written by a woman who was simply recorded as Mrs. Child, *The American Frugal Housewife* was marketed as a compilation of suggestions for homemakers. Published in 1833 this guidebook was in circulation during the time leading up to the Civil War. *The Frugal Housewife* was "dedicated to those who are not ashamed of economy" and could be used as a recipe for any number of household activities. Among the many topics covered by Mrs. Child was the subject of illnesses and their treatments. Listed below are some bullet statements drawn from Mrs. Child's nostrums.

- Cotton wool, wet with sweet oil and paregoric, relieves the earache very soon.

- A good quantity of old cheese is the best thing to eat when distressed by eating too much fruit, or oppressed with any kind of food.
- Honey and milk is very good for worms.
- For a sudden attack of quincy or croup, bathe the neck with bear's grease, and pour it down the throat.
- Equal parts of camphor, spirits of wine, and hatshorn, well mixed, and rubbed upon the throat, is said to be good for the croup.
- Cotton wool and oil are the best things for a burn.
- A poultice of wheat bran, or rye bran, and vinegar, very soon takes down the inflammation occasioned by a sprain.
- In case of any scratch, or wound, from which the lock-jaw is apprehended, bathe the injured part freely with lye or pearl-ash and water.
- A rind of pork bound upon a wound occasioned by a needle, pin, or nail, prevents lock-jaw.
- Spirits of turpentine is good to prevent lock-jaw.
- If you happen to cut yourself while cooking, bind on some fine salt: molasses is also good.
- Flour boiled thoroughly in milk, so as to make quite a thick porridge, is good in cases of dysentery.
- Black or green tea, steeped in boiling milk, seasoned with nutmeg, and best of loaf sugar, is excellent for dysentery.
- Flannel wet with brandy, powdered with Cayenne pepper, and laid upon the bowels, affords great relief in cases of extreme dysentery distress.
- Whortleberries, commonly called huckleberries, dried, are a useful medicine for children. Made into tea, and sweetened with molasses, they are very beneficial, when the digestive system is in a restricted state, and the digestive powers out of order.

- Blackberries are extremely useful in cases of dysentery. To eat the berries is very healthy; tea made of the leaves and roots is very beneficial; and syrup made of the berries is still better. Blackberries have sometimes effected a cure when physicians despaired.
- Loaf sugar and brandy relieves a sore throat; when very bad, it is good to inhale the steam of scalding hot vinegar through the tube of a tunnel.
- A stocking bound on warm from the foot, at night, is good for a sore throat.
- An ointment made from the common ground-worms, which boys dig to bait fishes, rubbed on the hand, is said to be excellent, when the sinews are drawn up by any disease or accident.
- If a wound bleeds very fast, and there is no physician at hand, cover it with the scrapings of sole-leather, scraped like coarse lint.
- Balm-of-Gilead buds bottled up in N. E. rum, make the best cure in the world for fresh cuts and wounds. Every family should have a bottle of it.
- Half a spoonful of citric acid, (which may always be bought of the apothecaries) stirred in half a tumbler of water, is for the head-ache.
- Boiled potatoes are said to cleanse the hands as well as common soap.
- Water-gruel, with three or four onions simmered in it, prepared with a lump of butter, pepper, and salt, eaten just before one goes to bed, is said to be a cure for a hoarse cold.
- Nothing is so good to take down swellings, as a soft poultice of stewed white beans, put on a thin muslin bag, and renewed every hour or two.
- The thin white skin, which comes from suet, is excellent to bind upon the feet for chilblains.
- Always apply diluted laudanum to fresh wounds.

- Burnt alum held in the mouth is good for the canker.
- The common dark-blue violet makes a slimy tea, which is excellent for the canker.
- Tea made from slippery elm is good for the piles, and for humors in the blood.
- An ointment of lard, sulpher, and cream-of-tarter, simmered together, is good for the piles.
- The constant use of malt beer, or malt in any way, is said to be a preservative against fevers.
- Black cherry-root bark, barberry bark, mustard-seed, petty morrel-root, and horseradish, well steeped in cider, are excellent for the jaundice.
- A poultice made of ginger or common chickweed, that grows about one's door in the country, has given great relief to the tooth-ache, when applied frequently to the cheek.
- A spoonful of ashes stirred in cider is good to prevent sickness of the stomach.
- When a blister from a burn breaks it is said to be a good plan to put wheat flour upon the naked flesh.
- Vinegar curds, made by pouring vinegar into warm milk, put on warm and changed pretty frequently, are excellent to subdue inflammation.
- Chalk, wet with hartshorn is a remedy for the sting of a bee.
- Boil castor-oil with an equal quantity of milk, sweeten it with a little sugar, stir it well, and, when cold, give it to children for drink. They will never suspect it is medicine; and will even love the taste of it.
- Whiskey that has had Spanish-flies soaking in it is said to be good for ring-worms.
- It is worthwhile to mention what is best to be done for the bite of a rattlesnake—Cut the flesh out, around the bite, *instantly*; that the poison may not have time to circulate in the blood. If caustic is at hand, put it upon the

raw flesh; if not, the next best thing is to fill the wound with salt—renewing it occasionally. Take a dose of sweet oil and spirits of turpentine, to defend the stomach. If the whole limb swells, bathe it in salt and vinegar freely. It is well to physic the system thoroughly before returning to usual diet.

In looking back at these household remedies one can come away with a clearer understanding of what common folk thought worked as medicinal cures. Each of these prescriptions was applied with some regularity when people were confronted with illness or injury. How well they worked is open to debate but the fact remains that *The American Frugal Housewife* was a publication that had some longevity. Published through twelve editions by 1833 it remained on bookshelves for generations as a well-worn and tattered resource book. The ideas it contained about simple first aid must have had a broad application. Therefore, by looking back at some of these common sense or odd remedies we better grasp what every day people of the Civil War era did when confronted by health concerns.

Source

Mrs. Child, *The American Frugal Housewife*, Chapman Billies, Inc., Sandwich, MA
    1833, ISBN: 0-939218-2

– Chapter 19 –

Fielding Questions: Tips to Reenactors

You are sitting in camp on a hot summer day. Sweat is running down inside your woolen uniform. Nearby, a campfire is burning and coffee is on to boil. All of a sudden a few spectators come by and gape at you. One of the braver souls walks up to you and your comrades and asks the seemingly proverbial question, "Are those clothes hot?" After being assured that wool, when exposed to summer heat, is a warm fabric, the seemingly hapless spectator follows up with a second question, "Is that a real fire?"

If you have been a reenactor for any length of time you will have been approached by members of the viewing public who invariably ask questions of varying degrees of depth, breadth, and value. While the situation described in the introduction to this piece may seem exaggerated, in reality it is all too common. When working with the public it is essential to realize that not everyone has the same interest, depth of knowledge, or common sense as is the norm. How a reenactor handles questions, even when they are rather odd, is a test of their mettle as a living historian.

Over the past year I have seen strands on popular online reenactor forums that have featured topics such as "What was the stupidest question you were ever asked as a reenactor?" While, at first blush, some of the types of questions that reenactors encounter are superficial at best, it is counterproductive to demean any sincere question. The person who asked about how warm woolen uniforms were was probably not the most perceptive person out there. However, such a seemingly obvious question may simply represent a person who sincerely wants to interact with people who are doing something very novel but does not know where to begin the conversation. Likewise, a superficially "silly" question may be asked by a person who struggles with shyness or their innate capacities. We honor nobody, least of all the folks we represent as living historians, if we allow the surface oddness of a question to lead us to discourteous, sneering, or supercilious behavior.

In that spirit, what follows are ten practical suggestions for dealing with questions both at events and during presentations in places such as schools or with community groups. The emphasis in each section is on highlighting strategies to improve communication while also making it more fun to work with the public. Remember, if you really are a living historian, part and parcel of your assignment is to interact with people, to teach, and to learn.

1. *Listen Carefully*

There is an ancient Taoist question that may be of great value to people who work with the public, "Are you listening, or merely waiting to speak?" All too often people cannot wait for their next turn in a conversation and in so doing miss everything that other people are saying. When a person is asking you about your musket, various bits of equipment, or any aspect of Civil War life focus on the questioner and not on what you are about to say. If you can focus your attention on the person or people with whom your are conversing you stand a far better chance of both answering their questions and establishing a positive rapport. Listening is an art as well as the responsibility of anyone who presents themselves as a living historian.

2. *Be Concise*

The famed writer Oscar Wilde once gave the following advice to speakers, "Be short, be brief, be seated." Brevity can be much more productive than a response that flows on and on. This fact is especially noteworthy when presenting to children. Youngsters' attention spans vary both due to age and development. An answer that swirls around, about, and over the original question may well lose the audience even though it impresses the speaker. Listen to the question that is being asked, answer in a thorough yet concise manner, and then restate a key point or two to guarantee understanding. By being short and to the point a speaker will be able to increase the amount of dialog and exchange that occurs during a presentation or conversation. If you take five to ten minutes to answer a question that really does not leave much time for other people to speak and/or learn.

3. *Stick to the Facts*

If you have a great depth of knowledge and you know your audience well it is safer to venture into the world of opinion and conjecture. However, the risk you run in presenting too much information laced with your personal opinions is that the objectivity of your presentation may be flawed. There are some very controversial topics that are associated with the Civil War. For example, if you are presenting to students who are ethnically diverse and you make the debatable statement, "Slavery wasn't the real cause of the Civil War", you stand a very real chance of creating rancor and misunderstanding. In that example, while the speaker may well feel justified in making that debatable claim; it is unfair to impose one perspective upon an impressionable audience. By sticking to the facts a speaker can be fairer to the uninitiated listener while also serving a more educationally balanced purpose. If you wish to present controversial facts then be sure to dedicate some time to opposing perspectives. An example of this might be discussing the pros and cons of the controversy attendant to the display of the Confederate flag. If you only show one side of an issue are you educating or propagandizing?

4. Be Culturally Sensitive

We live in a world that is increasingly interconnected and diverse. When you go to a living history event or venture forth into classrooms you stand a good chance of encountering people of diverse cultural backgrounds. The way you handle questioners should reflect sensitivity to the differences that exist in people's backgrounds. For example, if you go to a school to do a presentation and many of the youngsters are Hispanic you may need to adjust your presentation and demeanor because of the simple fact that the group's understanding of American history could be radically different than your own. Likewise, the questions from a group of urban African-American youngsters may revolve around slavery or the role of Blacks in the Civil War to a much greater extent than those raised in a rural predominantly Caucasian school. A good performer or speaker knows their audience and adapts their performance to them. Part of knowing your audience is being sensitive to the divergent levels of understanding that different people bring to a presentation.

5. Use Developmentally Appropriate Language

Stephen Covey, a leading guru in the field of human behavior and management, once said, "Seek to understand; and then to be understood." If we can try to grasp where other people are coming from we stand a much better chance of actually communicating with them. In this context a major element of being understood is to select words that match your audience. The most profound answer featuring complex tactical breakdowns and a vivid description of a general's leadership style may be wasted if the audience does not understand your presentation. Likewise, talking down to people can be symptomatic of underestimating your audience. Such an approach may alienate those with whom you are speaking and certainly will lose their interest. In those instances when you present in schools bear in mind the age and interest level of the students. "Hands on" approaches may be better with younger children that with high schoolers. At the elementary level, the use of too much verbal language rather than visuals may be a mismatch. Conversely, if you are presenting at a Civil War roundtable be prepared because the attendees probably are passionate and knowledgeable about this topic. Match what you say with who is listening, their interest level, and their experiences.

6. Honor Every Question

There really are very few stupid questions, but there can be impatient, irritating, or arrogant responses to inquiries. If a person has taken the time to come out to an event, slogged through mud, or battled the heat it is your responsibility to at least be patient when they ask you an ill informed question. People who see ill-conceived or superficial questions as stupid and beneath their dignity to answer are really rather snobbish in their attitude. A rather simple question can be transformed into a positive circumstance if the person asking it is honored. For example, the classic, "Were the monuments here when the battle was fought?" question can be made in a workable communication exercise by being patient. Instead of smirking at the questioner a person could say, "No, the monuments were added years later. In fact the people who paid for the monuments often fought in the battle and were lucky enough to have survived it. Do you have any idea how many soldiers fought here and how many died?" By being sensitive, patient, and creative in your response you can make a person feel welcome rather than sneering at them. The person asking a seemingly arcane question probably does not intend to merely irritate you. He or she is interested enough to take a risk and ask you for information. Be kind and remember you too did not always know what you know about this, or any other, subject.

7. *__Be Courteous__*

There are rude and discourteous people all over the place. Yet, if someone else is thoughtless that does not provide you with a license to follow suit. You will meet people at events or in classrooms who are rude. When faced with a confrontive or know-it-all mentality it behooves you to become even more courteous than you normally would. By taking the high road you show, through your personal example, that discourse can be civil. I remember one school presentation when a particular student interrupted me every five minutes or so with what appeared to be smart aleck types of comments. Ironically, when the time came to load gear back into my vehicle it was this youngster who volunteered to help me pack my stuff out. En route to my car, when we were one-on-one the lad had some very interesting questions about my weapon and gear.

Amazingly, several years later this lad became a reenactor and served in the field with me as a good comrade. By being courteous you can plant seeds of kindness and understanding rather than accentuating the negative.

8. *Focus on the Questioner*

A strong presenter realizes that the success of the presentation is dependent upon two key things. First, the speaker must understand not only the material he or she is presenting but also how to offer information in an entertaining and effective manner. Second, the presenter needs to connect with the audience and thereby bring out the best in them as well. One key element to connection is simply paying attention to the attitude of the people to whom you are presenting. Watch for the non-verbal behavior of the audience. If the people watching you are restless or distracted that is a sure sign that you are missing the mark in some way. Similarly, when somebody asks you a question focus your attention upon that individual. By truly hearing and seeing what a person asks, you will be better prepared to answer in a meaningful manner. If you pay attention to the people around you it will be amazing how much more fully you and they will appreciate your time together. Sometimes questions can seem repetitive. How many times can you explain the loading procedure for an Enfield rifled musket before it becomes commonplace to you? However, always remember that your presentation probably is the first of its kind that members of your audience have seen. Be at your best and who knows what affect you will have on others.

9. *Avoid Argumentativeness*

There are certain issues in American society that can trigger emotional rather than rational debate. Topics such as abortion, capital punishment, and religious differences all are ones that may well engender sparks of discord among people of differing persuasions. In terms of the Civil War, certain subjects also carry with them more of an emotional edge than others. The legality of secession, slavery as a cause of the war, the atrocities committed in certain prisons, the justness of various causes all can trigger sharp debate amongst Civil War fans. In the correct context such debate is appropriate and even fun. However, during a presentation such debate can spin out of control and lead to argument rather than discourse. There is a clear line between how strongly you can disagree and manifest disagreement in a public presentation. In a school situation you can rely upon the classroom teacher to step in and handle any disciplinary issues that occur. But, if you are talking to a group of spectators and debate rages over a subject such as "the numerous Black soldiers who served in the Rebel armies" then discretion might be the best defense. I once watched a learned comrade-in-arms patiently attempt to disabuse an obviously racist spectator of his opinions regarding the value of USCT troops. Eventually my friend simply said, "Sir, you are misinformed and I am not going to be able to help you right now." My friend then walked away and sought out other people to converse with. Argumentation in public can be ugly and ill advised. Conversely, you need not simply stay around and absorb the arrogance, ignorance, or discourtesy of people who happen to wander into your Civil War orbit.

10. Restate/Rephrase/Reinforce

When a person asks you a question in a large group situation it is often a good idea to restate or paraphrase their question prior to answering it. Such a restating of the question accomplishes several important goals. To begin, by restating the question you are making it more likely that other members of the audience heard and attended to it. Secondly, such a repeat of the question assures that no misinterpretation of it on your part has occurred. Finally, by taking the time to restate the original question you demonstrate your attentiveness and concern for the questioner. Rephrasing can also help to "clean up" a somewhat cumbersome albeit well in tended question. If, for example, a person jumbles up his or her question about the culinary habits of soldiers, you might say, "Let me see if I understand what you are asking—you are interested in knowing what soldiers typically ate and how they made their food? That's really an excellent question and one I was hoping somebody would ask." The use of positive reinforcement by a speaker helps win over the audience and offers sincere praise for people brave enough to venture a question. If you are positive in how you handle questions you increase the likelihood of more and better involvement on the part of the audience. Such connection should lead to a much more mutually satisfying exchange and better memories. It takes very little time to couch a question in a positive manner. Why not help make someone's day by not only presenting fascinating information but also leaving them with a fond memory of the situation?

Closing Remarks

In closing, there are some reenactors who feel either uncomfortable or overly confident when they present to others about their beloved hobby and the time period they recreate. Sometimes, a reenactor could not only do a better job of presenting but also feel more fulfilled by speaking to others through the use of some basic communication strategies. In other instances, a person who is overconfident about their specialized knowledge would do well to be more aware of the nature, interest, and needs of the audience to whom they are presenting. The act of communicating is a complex one indeed. Through the give and take of active listening and engagement with people, you stand a much better chance of connecting with others and also imparting some of the passion and knowledge you have about America's Civil War. Is that not a reason for taking all the time and energy necessary to stage a decent presentation? If so, please make the effort needed to read others and offer them a living history memory that will last and inspire.

– Chapter 20 –

Reenactor's Bookshelf: Ten Civil War Artillery Books Worth Reading

The Civil War was fought across four years and many theaters of operations. Over the years, historians have paid great attention and homage to the men and women who lived during those war years. Thousands of books have been printed dealing with virtually every aspect of the war. Yet, while there are numerous high quality biographies, battle monographs, studies in command, and social histories dealing with multiple aspects of the war years there remain relatively few books about artillery. In many ways this dearth of reading material about the "long arm" of the armed services should not be surprising. The artillery, although a powerful force on the battlefield has been a relative "step child" both in the research and day-to-day practical world of the military. One need only consider the ambivalent way that artillery batteries are now typically used in reenactments to understand the fashion in which that important branch of the military was overlooked in the 1860's.

What follows are concise summaries and reviews of ten books that are available and worth perusing if you wish to better understand the role, function, and experiences of Civil War artillerymen. Hopefully, by taking a look at some of these works readers will not only have a better historical base for understanding the important roles filled by artillerists during the Civil War but also why artillery reenactors have such a unique role in the events they take part in. Therefore, what follows below is a simple roadmap to reading about a subject that may be either new territory or review for readers but will certainly underscore how much artillerymen contributed to both Union and Confederate war efforts.

Another point to bear in mind if you consider reading these texts is that maintaining & increasing your knowledge of the Civil War is essential for several reasons. First, if you wish to understand the events of the war better you will have to study. Second, the more you know about the many aspects of the Civil War the more knowledge you can pass on to students and other spectators who may encounter you at a reenactment. Next, reading can help you to develop more empathy & understanding of the people who lived during the Civil War. Finally, reading is an act of growth—when we read and learn we stay alive. Therefore, for these, and many other reasons, it is hoped that these artillery bookshelf suggestions will be of value to you. Of course, similar lists could be structured for infantry, cavalry, naval issues, and other aspects of the Civil War. That being the case perhaps you should expand your reading into those areas and learn along the way.

Cannons: An Introduction to Civil War Artillery
Dean Thomas

In *Cannons* author and publisher Dean Thomas offers readers a concise and illustrated introduction to the world of Civil War ordnance. The author begins by detailing the types of projectiles and fuses that Civil War artillerymen used on the battlefield. Then, the individual types of light, heavy, and siege artillery pieces that would most commonly have been used by the competing armies are presented. In each instance artillery pieces are described in terms of their unique capabilities and uses. Each entry is accompanied by illustrations from the period or via modern photos. Specific technical information such as bore size, tube material, length & weight of the piece, range, and powder charge are also listed out for each cannon. Thus, readers are provided an excellent and concise reference book through which they can receive a quick education about the way in which Civil War artillery and ordnance was used. Thomas does an outstanding job of affording his readers a good look at weapons such as the 1857 12-Pounder, Field Howitzers, Parrott Rifles, mortars, and the 3-Inch Ordnance Rifle. For either an artillery novice or an experienced student Thomas' book will provide insights and explanations that will be of value. *1995, Gettysburg, PA: Thomas Publications, $6.95, 72 pp., ISBN: 0-9396931-03-2*

Double Canister At Ten Yards
David Shultz

Perhaps no more memorable moment occurred during the Civil War than Pickett's Charge. On the third day of fighting at Gettysburg Meade's Federals stopped the Confederate forces of Robert E. Lee's Army of Northern Virginia. The doomed assault by Pickett's men was, to a very large extent, stymied due to the effectiveness and lethality of the Federal artillerists. Here, in David Shultz's concise study of the Federal artillery at Gettysburg readers will be given a description of that defensive action that they will remember. Shultz writes with the style of a novelist but also grounds his work on solid research. The text of this rapid paced work includes numerous quotes from soldier's letters, diaries, and reports. In many ways Shultz's work tells two parallel stories. On the one hand the author relates the way in which this major defensive victory impacted the average cannoneers who served in the Army of the Potomac. On the other hand, Shultz's excellent little book tells the tale of General Henry Hunt, the Union artillery commander at Gettysburg. Hunt, a brilliant officer who was often overlooked in his day, was a pivotal figure in the Federal victory. Hunt's wise use of men and resources linked to his

personal bravery helped gird the loins of the Union gunners. In the end, it was Hunt's strategy that, to a large extent, crushed the Confederate assault. Yet, despite the abilities of Hunt and his artillerists, the tide of battle did sweep up to the "high water mark." As is noted in the title of this fine book, Confederate soldiers were met by Federal gunners working in Cowan's Battery, with "Double canister at ten yards." That ferocity of struggle helped defeat the brave Rebel foes and also served as an excellent title for a book that will offer its readers both valuable information and a well written narrative. *1995, Redondo Beach, CA: Rank and File Publications, $9.95,*
(77 pp.), ISBN: 0-9638-993-5-X

Behind the Guns: The History of Battery I, 2nd Regiment Illinois Light Artillery
Thaddeus C.S. Brown, Samuel J. Murphy, & William G. Putney
Clyde C. Walton (Ed.)

While much has been written about the infantry and cavalry units that fought during the Civil War relatively few primary source artillery unit histories exist. In this fascinating book the history of Battery I, 2nd Illinois Light Artillery is reprinted in a way that will engage the interest of most Civil War enthusiasts. In its day Battery I was a standard Western Federal artillery unit. Its members came from Northern Illinois with a particularly large cadre that mustered in from Joliet. The battery was a solid outfit and one that was destined to see hard service. The men of Battery I were engaged in combat at Perryville, Chickamauga, and Atlanta. Battery I also was a unit that made the "March to the Sea" under the tutelage of General Sherman. In this book some of the men who were members of Battery unit recount not only the chronological events of the unit but also quite a number of interesting anecdotes and vignettes. Readers who take the time to peruse this book will come away with a much deeper understanding of what day-to-day life in a Civil War artillery outfit was like. Accounts of camp life, disease, boredom, pranks, power struggles, personality conflicts, and loneliness abound in the pages of this work. Also included are vivid depictions of what combat was like for these artillerists. In the end, Battery I's men returned to the towns, cities, and farms of Illinois. They left behind the wartime experiences they wished to discard and carried with them the memories and physical reminders of the war they had seen. They also left behind a striking history of the Civil War told from the perspective of their wonderful unit history and one that tells a story rare among the pantheon of Civil War books. *2000, Carbondale, IL: Southern Illinois University Press, $16.95 (180 pp.), ISBN: 0-8093-2342-7*

The Man Behind the Guns: A Military Biography of General Henry J. Hunt
Edward G. Longacre

During the course of the Civil War few Federal officers made as great a contribution as General Henry J. Hunt. As commander of the Army of the Potomac's artillery General Hunt had great responsibility. An officer who possessed both great skill and bravery, Hunt was in the apex of battle on many fields. Perhaps nowhere was Hunt's contribution greater than at Gettysburg where he spearheaded the Union efforts to rebuff General Lee's various attacks. At the "high water mark" Hunt led the Federal artillerists who blunted General Pickett's powerful but ultimately doomed assault. On that day Hunt not only oversaw the Federal artillery force that crushed the Confederate attack but also took an active part in the battle itself. As the Rebel troops surged forward toward the low stone wall that marked the Federal line, Hunt fired his pistol

into the oncoming enemies. As he yelled, "See 'em! See 'em!" and fired his sidearm Hunt's horse was shot from under him. Pinned beneath his steed Hunt spied the oncoming Union relief force that eventually stemmed the Rebel tide. Yet, while this may have been the most perilous and memorable moment in Hunt's Civil War service it was not unique for a man who led at the front. In this biography readers will come to know a man who served his nation well. A veteran of both the Mexican and Civil War Henry Hunt was a first rate soldier. However, due to a tendency to run afoul of controversy, Hunt was never afforded either the recognition or rank he deserved. Acrimony with people such as Grant, Sherman, Hancock, and President Chester Arthur all stymied the advancement of Hunt's career. When he died 1n 1888 Hunt was a relatively poor man with a large family. He had served his nation as a preeminent soldier and the "soul of the artillery." Sadly, much of Hunt's contribution is relatively little known to casual students of the Civil War. This thoroughly researched and carefully written work by Edward G. Longacre is a valuable tool in the cause of understanding Henry Hunt, a complex and capable soldier.
2003, Cambridge, MA: Da Capo Press, $18.00, (294 pp.), ISBN: 0-306-81154-5

Artillery Hell: The Employment of Artillery at Antietam
Curt Johnson & Richard C. Anderson, Jr.

During the Battle of Antietam Union artillery batteries were in a position to exact a great toll from their Confederate counterparts. In a battle where the Rebel gunners were under orders to primarily focus upon Federal infantry formations rather than counter-battery fire the cost to the Confederate artillerists was steep. Time and again, Union batteries would concentrate their fire upon Confederate artillery positions and wreck their guns. On the other hand, Confederate artillerists helped to stem the tide of battle at places such as the Dunker Church and the Bloody Lane. Here, in *Artillery Hell,* the technical side of the battle of Antietam from an artillery perspective is presented. In this book readers will have the opportunity to review a series of short to moderately long essays dealing with the role and positioning of artillery at the battle that produced more casualties in a single day than any other event in American history. The centerpiece essay is one crafted by the Head NPS ranger assigned to Antietam in 1940. Also included are shorter selections that address the nature of Civil War artillery pieces & their ordnance, artillery tactics, the movements of each individual battery on the field of battle, and summative reports from various Federal battery commanders. In the end, readers with an eye for technical detail will come away from this book with a resource volume that can be used to pinpoint the exact role every artillery battery engaged at Antietam filled. While, due to its technical nature, this is not a book for every reader it does offer up valuable information that a harder core artillery enthusiast will find enlightening. Of particular interest is the final section that includes battery reports from Federal artillery commanders. In those post-battle summations the Union artillery officers who waged the battle of Antietam offer insights into the very reason why that struggle was referred to as "Artillery Hell." *1995, College Station, TX: Texas A & M University Press, $14.95, (144 pp.), ISBN: 0-89096-623-0*

4 Years In The Confederate Artillery: The Diary of Pvt. Henry Robinson Berkeley
Henry Robinson Berkeley
William H. Runge (Ed.)

   In 1861 Henry Robinson Berkeley became one of the hundreds of thousands of American citizens who volunteered to fight in what was to become our Civil War. Berkeley was a decent and literate man who maintained a diary throughout his four years of service. As a member of the as a member of the *Hanover Artillery,* Henry Robinson Berkeley saw action in some of the bloodiest battles of the entire war. Berkeley, and his fellow Virginians in the battery, fought under the overall command of Robert E. Lee. Latter in the war, Berkeley and his battery mates were detached to become part of General Jubal Early's invasion force that swept north to the gates of Washington City. Subsequently, in the later stages of General Early's ignominious effort to defend the Shenandoah Valley, Berkeley was captured by Federal troops. For four months Berkeley was held captive by the Federals only to return home after taking the required loyalty oath. During the war Henry Berkeley was a tried and true soldier. His diary yielded glimpses into Berkeley's perceptions on combat, living conditions in camp, the arduous nature of being on the march, the devastation of war, and the human kindness that even the horrors of war could not fully suppress. Indeed, it is the very decency of Henry Robinson Berkeley that shines through the pages of this revealing diary. Simply put, Henry Robinson Berkeley was a man who joined the Confederate Army due to deeply held principles. Berkeley fought for four years and suffered mightily in defense of a cause that he never fully understood. However, the bonds of comradeship that were forged in the fiery furnace of battle kept Berkeley true to his commitment. In the end, despite the defeat of his cause Henry Berkeley remained steadfast in his belief that, "there is something deep within me that tells me plainly that it was not all passed through in vain." In the diary that Henry Berkeley left to his family there remains the story of one artilleryman whose individual wartime experiences made up a part of the whole cloth we know as the Civil War. This is an excellent book and one, despite its out-of-print status, that can be located for purchase via *Amazon* or other on-line sources. *1991,*

Richmond, VA: The Virginia Historical Society, $10.00, (156 pp.), ISBN: 0-945015-05-4

Cushing at Gettysburg: The Story of a Union Artillery Commander
Kent Masterson Brown

For students of the Gettysburg Campaign, Alonzo Cushing remains one of the more memorable junior officers of those momentous days. As commander of Battery A, 4th US Artillery, Cushing was posted to a spot near the epicenter of the Gettysburg Battle. Stationed at the angle of the famous stonewall, Cushing and his men were at the very center of the Union line. There, on July 3, 1863 the Confederate brigade commanded by Lewis Armistead attempted to smash through the Federal defense line. In that eventful engagement, Cushing commanded an artillery battery that both exacted a great cost from their foes while also suffering terrible losses. During the battle, Cushing was shot in his shoulder and then suffered a terrible wound to his lower abdomen and private parts. Despite these painful injuries and the disablement of four of his six cannons, Cushing remained at his post for ninety minutes. Finally, as the Confederate troops of Pickett's division surged to the very edge of the Union position, Cushing ordered the firing of a final round from his depleted section of guns. At that moment, Alonzo Cushing was struck below the nose with a Rebel ball. He fell into the arms of his trusted comrade, First Sergeant Frederick Fuger. A veteran of all the major battles fought by the Army of the Potomac, Cushing died then and there on the field of battle. Eventually, Cushing's body was buried at his beloved West Point where visitors continue to come and look at the final resting place of a young and capable Federal artillery officer. The story of Alonzo Cushing, and the branch of service he volunteered for, is ably told in this well researched biography. Author Kent Masterson Brown tells the story of a young Midwesterner who served bravely for a cause he believed in. Author Brown does a fine job of not only encapsulating Cushing's life but also telling the story of the artillery as it was in the bygone days of the Civil War. This is a solid book that reaches its apex in the prose used to describe the desperate days at Gettysburg. *1993, Lexington, KY: The University Press of Kentucky, $22.95, (330 pp.), ISBN: 0-8131-1837-9*

From Selma to Appomattox: The History of the Jeff Davis Artillery
Lawrence R. Laboda

While there are many unit histories dedicated to the infantry and cavalry, very few have been written about specific artillery formations. Here, in *From Selma to Appomattox,* author Lawrence R. Laboda provides a look at the Civil War world of one Confederate artillery battery. The Jeff Davis Artillery was raised in Alabama at the outset of the war. Made up of a mixture of Alabamian society the Jeff Davis Battery was destined to have a long and hard tour of duty. The men of this battery were dispatched east to become a part of General Lee's Army of Northern Virginia. As such the Jeff Davis Battery was fated to fight at most of the major engagements of the Eastern Theater. During its wartime service the men of the Jeff Davis Artillery suffered a very high rate of casualties. At Spotsylvania, for example, during the fight at "The Mule Shoe" the unit was overrun and lost both most of its ordnance and many of its men. Indeed, it was the hard luck of this unit to be involved in very close combat on several occasions with attendant casualties and captures on their part. In the end, due to attrition, the members of the Jeff Davis Artillery found themselves to have no more than a section of guns dispersed into other batteries. Those hearty members who had served through to the war's end had the grim opportunity to lay down their few remaining arms at Appomattox. However, despite their ultimate defeat, the Alabama men who served in a unit named after their commander-in-chief did well in defense of the cause they believed in. In this exhaustive unit history, that story is retold in a way that is eye opening. Not only are the major battles and culminating events touched upon. Rather, the author of this well researched volume tells the story of the day-to-day grind that Civil War life was for the soldiers who waged it. Although this is not a book written in the sprightly style of a novel it is a solid history of an artillery battery that fought and marched its way across the Civil War years. *1994, New York, NY: Oxford University Press, $16.95, (385 pp.), ISBN: 0-19-510997-X*

A Concise Guide to the Artillery at Gettysburg
Gregory A. Coco

Did you know that over 630 cannons were used at Gettysburg? Were you aware that only one 6-Pounder was deployed on that field of battle? Do you know that at 400 yards a bolt from a ten-pound Parrott Rifle could penetrate nearly six feet of wood? Can you name the Union artillerist who survived a premature ignition of a round despite his receiving over fifty wounds? These, and many other fascinating questions, can be answered after reading this concise look at the broad topic of the use of artillery during the climactic battle at Gettysburg. Author Gregory Coco who has produced a number of fine and readable Civil War texts provides readers a quick look at the way in which artillery was utilized by both sides at Gettysburg. Coco begins by offering a brief history of the evolution of artillery as a branch of service. Then, the author details the way in which specific artillery batteries were used by each corps engaged during the battle. This summary of action is followed by a helpful statistical look at the casualties and ordnance expended by every battery that fought at Gettysburg. Finally, the author provides a brief analysis of the types of cannons and ordnance typically used in July of 1863. Taken as a whole, this book will provide readers with an interest in both artillery and the Gettysburg Campaign some useful information. While this book is not written in quite the same anecdotal style as some of Coco's other books it does hit the mark in terms of content. This is a book that readers should bring with them when they next visit the Gettysburg National Military Park as it has a wealth of information that can only add to such an experience. *1998, Gettysburg, PA: Thomas Publications, $10.00, (96 pp.), ISBN: 1-57747-012-5*

American Civil War Artillery, 1861-1865: Field Artillery
Philip Katcher

During the Civil War field artillery became a vital branch of service. The field or "light" artillery batteries that served across all fronts generally provided excellent support to their far more numerous infantry cousins. However, in the Confederate armies, artillery, while ably manned, was dogged by inadequacies of ordnance. Decreased industrial supports on the homefront resulted in shells, shot, powder, and fuses that were of uneven quality. As a result, for example, Rebel infantrymen were far less enamored of the idea of their artillerists firing over their positions at distant Yankees as, all too often, Confederate ordnance prematurely detonated at the expense of their own men. Conversely, Union artillerists faced no such barriers to success. By and large, Federal gunners had the finest weaponry and ordnance then available. Additionally, leavened by a number of regular army cannoneers at the outset of the war, Union artillery batteries became one of the most professional and capable sectors of the Northern armies. From the beginning to the end of the war blue-clad gunners served not only their pieces but also their nation at a top-flight level of performance. In *American Civil War Artillery* Philip Katcher provides an illustrated overview of how field guns and the men who manned them functioned during the conflict in question. Katcher begins by detailing the organizational structure of the two opposing artillery forces. Then, the author describes the types of fuses and projectiles most commonly available during the four war years. Finally, Katcher offers concise descriptions of the most common, and a few unique, light artillery pieces that may have traversed the battlefields of the Civil War. In this helpful book readers will learn about the workmanlike guns such as the 12-pdr. Napoleon, the 10 and 20-pdr. Parotts, and the 3-inch Ordnance Rifle. Additionally, unusual guns such as the Whitworth and Wiard Rifles are also touched upon. As part of the *Osprey Publications* series of military titles Katcher's book is both typically well written and technically informative. The inclusion of numerous drawings, prints, and period photographs also does a great deal to amplify the extensive information contained in this work. This is a good book for readers with an interest in Civil War artillery and the way in which it was used. *2001, Wellingborough, Northants: UK, $14.95, (48 pp.),* ISBN: *1-84176-218-0*

– Chapter 21 –

Women Warriors: A Sourcebook for Women Who Wish to Portray a Civil War Soldier

In August of 1861 at Lancaster, Ohio an eighteen-year-old student enlisted for three years in the 17th Ohio. The lad was named Private Frank Deming and was described as five feet six inches tall, with a dark complexion, gray eyes, and black hair. Private Deming served in the 17th until May 18, 1862 when he was discharged for disability at Corinth, Mississippi. Deming's certificate of discharge noted that he was unfit for duty for "no days" during the past two months. Further, unit records indicated that Private Deming had faithfully completed his duties as a soldier during his entire nine months service. Nevertheless Deming's discharge papers stated that he was "incapable of performing the duties of a soldier" because of "a congenital peculiarity which should have prevented…admission into the Army." That specific "congenital peculiarity was Private Deming's "being a female." The company clerk dutifully noted on the next muster roll that Deming's "disability" was "being a woman." No further records regarding Frank Deming exist but what is known is that she served in the Civil War just like an untold number of other women warriors.

In our own day and age a continuing controversy exists regarding the appropriateness of women reenactors in the military ranks. For some male reenactors the presence of a woman in the ranks, regardless of the quality of her impression, is anathema. For others, a more tolerant attitude prevails. Whatever the flavor of the units a woman may wish to join, it is important that she have a firm understanding of the historical realities as existed regarding women in the actual ranks of Civil War military units in the north and south. Perhaps the best sourcebook of information concerning the realities of women Civil War soldiers is *They Fought Like Demons* by Deann Blanton & Lauren Cook. If a woman is interested in pursuing a military impression it is highly recommended that she read this book. Likewise, male reenactors who wish to more fully understand what women soldiers experienced from 1861-65 should peruse the pages of this well written, thoroughly researched, and fascinating book.

They Fought Like Demons chronicles the story of the women soldiers who served on both sides during the American Civil War. Written with style, grace, and a researcher's eye, this book tells a fascinating and overlooked story of the war. The authors have exhaustively searched through a variety of primary and secondary sources to craft a compelling and unbiased look at one of the stranger and more misunderstood phenomena of the Civil War. In telling this story the authors delve into questions regarding women Civil War soldiers that have remained either unanswered or ignored for far too long. As such this anecdote filled monograph will add to the understanding of even the most avid student of Civil War history. This is an engaging subject and one that DeAnne Blanton and Lauren M. Cook do and outstanding job of tackling.

In terms of why women secretively joined both the Union and Confederate forces the authors note that there were many explanations. On the one hand, many women, north & south, felt the same patriotic surge that drove their male counterparts to enlist at the outset of the war. Many women who did not ultimately attempt to surreptitiously join the respective armies lamented their inability to do so. Cordelia Scales of South Carolina recorded in her wartime journal, "It seems so hard that we who have the wills of men should be denied from engaging in this great struggle for liberty just because we are ladies." Lucy Breckenridge, another southern woman, wrote the following diatribe, "I would gladly shoulder my pistol and shoot some Yankees if it were allowable...if some few southern women were in the ranks they would set the men an example they would not blush to follow." In the same vein, Sarah Morgan of Louisiana sorrowfully scribed, "O! If I was only a man! Then I could...slay them with a will."

Strong feelings such as those noted above were only a hop, skip, and a jump away from coaxing a cadre of strong-willed women to take the next steps of disguise and enlistment. Many such women felt great pride not only in their nation but also in their personal act of service and sacrifice. Years after the end of the Civil War Martha Lindley who had served as a "cavalryman" without notice wrote, "I did the best I could in the service of my country...I am only a woman, I think I can say without egotism that there were worse soldiers than I in the service."

This theme of pride in their service was common among the female warriors that either were discovered during their service or admitted to it after the war. For women who joined the ranks due to patriotic fervor their military service was as much a high point or calling as it was for their male comrades. Sarah Edmonds who wrote about her service in the Union Army described her attitude toward it in the following way, "I could only thank God that I was free and could go forward and work, and I was not obliged to stay at home and weep."

Another reason noted by the authors of this compelling book was the reality that perhaps only by imitating a man could a woman assure herself of any hope of economic independence. At the time of the Civil War women were thought of as property and not fiscal equals by men. Therefore, some women sought out male identities in order to garner work and earn a living. The thirteen dollars per month that a common private was paid far exceeded what women in domestic service or factory work could expect to earn.

In this spirit of independence several women soldiers recorded their desires to be a full fledged and non-dependent person. Rosetta Wakeman who served as Lyons Wakeman in the 153rd New York, chronicled these feelings in a letter home to her family, "I am as independent as a hog on ice." Another female enlistee, Sophia Crider, was described in her local paper as having joined the army "in a wild spirit of adventure." Georgianna Peterman who joined a Confederate regiment was described by her former schoolteacher as a person for whom "plain country life was not enough for her ambition."

Other reasons for military enlistment that the authors highlight include a search for adventure, personal revenge seeking, and following along with either family members or husbands. Indeed, a number of women who were discovered in the ranks were emotionally attached to other unit members and had followed them into service. Union Major William Ludlow reported encountering a Confederate prisoner during the 1864 Atlanta campaign who was a woman. This captured Confederate explained to Major Ludlow that "she belonged to the Missouri Brigade…had a husband and one or two brothers in one of the regiments, and followed them to war." All of this unnamed southern woman's relatives were killed during the war and, "having no home but the regiment," this female soldier "took a musket and served in the ranks."

In terms of women's ability to conceal their gender one need only recount the cursory at best medical examinations recruits were put through to understand how a well-disguised woman could enlist. Once in the service it was possible for women to conceal their identities under the generally poorly fitting uniforms of the day. Social customs during those days called for a fair amount of privacy and discretion. Blatant nakedness was uncommon so women would not have stood out as much as a modern reader might think. One need only recall Albert D.J. Cashier of the 95th Illinois to grasp the point that a woman could not only disguise herself as a soldier but also in civilian life as well. Cashier not only served without detection for three years but also successfully maintained a male persona until she was discovered in 1911.

One of the more interesting themes in this fine work is that of how woman soldiers were found out and subsequently treated. In many instances women were discovered as such after serious wounds, when they were captured, or after death on the battlefield. Several first hand accounts are cited in this work that recount the discovery of female soldiers among those killed on battlefields. For example, Private Mark Nickerson of the 10th Massachusetts Infantry recalled finding a dead Confederate woman at Antietam, "A sergeant in charge of a burying party from our regiment reported to his Captain that there was a dead Confederate up in the cornfield whom he had reason to believe was a woman. He wanted to know if she be kept separate, or brought along with the others. The Captain after satisfying himself that this Confederate was a woman ordered that she be buried by herself. The news soon spread among the soldiers that there was a woman among the Confederate dead, and many of them went and gazed upon the upturned face, and tears glistened in many eyes as they turned away. She was wrapped in a soldier's blanket and buried by herself and a headboard made from a cracker box was set up at her grave marked "unknown Woman CSA." Nothing in my experience up to that time affected me as did that incident. I wanted to know her history and why she was there. She must have been killed just as the Southerners were being driven back from the cornfield."

In a few unusual cases the actual discovery of a soldier's gender was brought about by her giving birth to a child. Outlandish though it may seem, the authors record several examples of female soldiers being able to hide their gender even though they were pregnant. One New Jersey corporal's delivery was supervised by Colonel Adrian Root of the 94th New York. With tongue in cheek Colonel Root wrote home to his mother and described this unusual event, "When I was last on duty as General Officer of the Day I came across a very singular case of illness out on the picket line…a corporal of a New Jersey regiment who was on duty with the pickets complained of being unwell, but little notice was given to his complaints at first. His pain and other symptoms of severe indisposition increased, becoming so evident that his officers had him carried to a nearby farmhouse. There the worthy corporal was safely delivered of a fine, fat little recruit for the …regiment."

  Generally, once women were discovered to be such they were summarily discharged. In the Union Army many women soldiers were simply kicked out of camp regardless of where the army was. In a few cases women soldiers were arrested as suspected spies. Some discovered females were incarcerated for short periods of time until their true identities could be discerned. Apparently, in the Confederate Army, some women who were discovered continued their service as they had proven themselves as worthy of trust. Many women soldiers were considered insane and were scoffed at.

  Historically, the role of women soldiers in the Civil War has been viewed in different ways. Immediately after the war many women veterans were considered eccentric but worthy of respect for their service. Then, as decades passed, those same women soldiers were characterized as morally degenerate or mad. For over a century the role women played in the war was dismissed and tossed aside by historians. Only in the past decade or so has more serious research been undertaken on this exotic but fascinating subject.

Ultimately there is no way to actually know how many women served as Union or Confederate soldiers. The authors have deduced that more than three hundred verifiable cases can be tabulated. However, there certainly were many more women who were either never discovered or who died with their gender unnoted. To this day we would have no knowledge of such noteworthy female soldiers as Sarah Wakeman or Albert D.J. Cashier if fate had not allowed for common knowledge. In the same way many other women probably donned blue or gray uniforms and fought for the reasons they saw fit. In remembering their misunderstood service authors DeAnne Blanton and Lauren M. Cook have both unearthed a treasure trove of primary source information and told a story that needed telling. *They Fought Like Demons* as at the same time a work of scholarship and of sincere emotion worthy of attention. It is also a book that serves as a primer for modern women wishing to follow in the footsteps of those intrepid ladies who felt compelled to join the army and serve their respective countries as they saw fit.

Source

Blanton, Deanne & Cook, Lauren M. *They Fought Like Demons: Women Soldiers In the Civil War.* 2002, New York, NY: Vintage Books, 277 pp. $14.00 ISBN: 1-4000-3315-2

– Chapter 22 –

Top Picks for Younger Civil War Readers

When you present to a school group or talk to children and their parents during a Civil War reenacting event one of the questions that often comes up is, "Are there any good Civil War books you could recommend for children?" Every year there are dozens of titles published about the Civil War that target children and adolescents as their audience. Some of these books are mediocre and not worthy of the time it takes to read them. Many of these books are good but not really original or noteworthy in their presentation, substance, or subject matter. A few books are excellent and well worth perusing. And then, there are some books that come out that are not only outstanding but also worthy of long standing attention not only form younger readers but adults as well.

What follows are concise summaries and reviews of a baker's dozen such books. Each of these titles is one that I have read and found great value in. Every entry below contains not only a short critical essay but also pertinent facts such as cost, age level, publisher, publication date, and book identification number. In looking at this list the reader should bear in mind that books are a matter of taste. Certainly many much more qualified reviewers could well construct a radically different list. However, these thirteen books afford reenactors and younger readers a sound place to start.

1

The Long Road to Gettysburg
Jim Murphy

There have been many books written about Gettysburg but this stands out as one of the best ever penned for younger readers. Jim Murphy is a masterful historian with a wonderful touch at bringing the life of common folk to the reader. In this book Murphy sets the stage for this history of the battle at Gettysburg be initially focusing upon Lincoln's preparation for the November 19, 1863 delivery of a few appropriate remarks at the newly opening National Cemetery. Murphy fades back in time to the actual battle and centers his attention upon two young soldiers whose lives led them to Gettysburg as well. Confederate Lieutenant John Dooley is a nineteen-year-old officer in a Virginia regiment. Only 130 pounds Dooley appears frail but he is a battle hardened and respected company commander. A young man who supports the Southern way of life, inclusive of slavery, Dooley hopes that the invasion of the North will set the stage for a Confederate victory in the war. On the Federal side Murphy focuses in on Corporal Thomas Galway of an Ohio infantry regiment. Galway is an Irish immigrant and he knows prejudice on a first hand basis. For Thomas Galway the Civil War was a conflict aimed at opposing oppression. Galway marches to Gettysburg hoping that a Union victory will mark a time when greater tolerance and freedom will emerge in American society. Through a combination of selections from these two soldier's diaries as well as a wealth of other primary sources Murphy creates a stirring account of the three-day fight at Gettysburg, its aftermath, and the long-term effects of the battle. Murphy provides the reader a clear look into the world of Civil War soldiers fighting in what has come to be widely viewed as the high tide of the Confederacy and the turning point of the Civil War. This book also features numerous period maps,

photos, and illustrations. These pictorial representations make this a striking book. In the end Lieutenant Dooley, a member of General Pickett's ill-fated division, met defeat, wounding, and capture at Gettysburg. Thomas Galway helped repel Pickett's Charge and went on to a long life working to ameliorate human suffering. These two men's lives were so different yet became conjoined at Gettysburg. Ending with a review of Lincoln's Gettysburg Address, this is a book to read, re-read, and savor. 1995, Scholastic, Ages 10 7 Up, $7.95.
ISBN: 0-590-20236-7

2

Rifles for Watie
Harold Keith

      The war in the trans-Mississippi area was a confusing one. In places like Missouri, Kansas, and Indian Territory the war took on a brutal nature that was seldom matched in the east or deep south. The trans-Mississippi spawned such men as Quantrell and Bloody Bill Anderson. Atrocities committed by both sides made this much more of a "dirty war" than was the case in other sectors. Another unique feature of the trans-Mississippi fighting was the presence of a few Native-American units. On the southern side General Stand Watie stood out as a Native-American leader who served to the very end of the war as a Confederate commander. In this *Newberry Medal* book we are introduced to the strange sequence of events that made the fighting west of the Mississippi so convoluted. Through the eyes of sixteen-year-old Jeff Bussey we see both sides of the story. Initially Jeff musters in as an infantryman in a Kansas regiment. Jeff enlists to defend his family and their farm from the ravages of people such as Stand Watie and his Cherokee legion. Jeff learns that being a soldier is not a glorious endeavor. He marches through dust and mud. He sees his friends shot in battle or sick in camp. He fears for his own life as each day may be his last. Through a twist of fate, Jeff is able to join a tough group of cavalry scouts who ride behind enemy lines dressed in Rebel gear. While taking part in one scouting mission Jeff is forced to join in with a Confederate unit. While his secret identity is not discovered Jeff is forced to ride along with the Rebels. Over time Jeff comes to see that there are good men on both sides. This knowledge confuses Jeff and he is no longer sure which side he is on. Forced by circumstances to face the reality that neither side is completely good or evil Jeff comes to question why war was necessary at all. Laced with interesting values questions and an exciting narrative this book serves the reader well. It is an adventurous tale with believable characters. It also deals with a little known aspect of the Civil War in a fine way.

1987, Harper Trophy, Ages 10 & Up, $3.95. ISBN: 0-06-447030-X

3

The Red Badge of Courage
Stephen Crane

Born six years after the end of the war Stephen Crane was never a soldier. Although he lived only twenty-eight years Crane was able to produce some wonderful fiction. His most memorable tale is this book dealing with the Civil War experiences of young Henry Fleming. Born and raised on a farm in New York State Henry sees the coming of the Civil War as a great opportunity for adventure. He enlists in an infantry regiment and endures the boredom and tribulations of training to become a fighter. Henry sometimes wonders what he will do when he first experiences combat. Thoughts of potential cowardice merge with dreams of glory. Eventually, Henry and his regimental comrades meet their Rebel foes in a confusing battle that Crane based upon the actual fight at Chancellorsville in May 1863. Henry finds combat different than his naïve expectations. Men are shot and die. Wounded soldiers scream out in agony and the enemy appears remorseless. Henry finds himself running from the fight and then is thrown into the depths of despair. He wanders behind the lines and encounters other soldiers who are wounded, afraid, and dying. Eventually, Henry finds his way back to the regiment bloodied and confused. Through an interesting chain of circumstances Henry suffers no shame for his earlier flight. Indeed, he comes to the forefront in battle and earns his pride through acquiring a true "red badge of courage." In the form of Henry Fleming, Stephen Crane has given us a look at the inner thoughts of an adolescent serving as a Union soldier. Henry's inner monologue and his conversations with his fellow soldiers offer a realistic look at the effects of combat upon young men. Henry sought personal worthiness through glory. In the end he found that war was truly destructive in its myriad of permutations. However, by doing his duty and placing the needs of his comrades above his own he comes away changed in both good and bad ways. This literary classic continues to be one of the best known fictional accounts of Civil War combat. 1995, Aerie Books, Ages 12 & Up, $4.95. ISBN: 1-55902-983-8

4

Brady
Jean Fritz

    Brady Minton is a young boy growing up in rural Pennsylvania at a time when life was increasingly complex. Living with his father who is a Protestant minister opposed to slavery, Brady is unsure of his own feelings about that grave question. Brady's mother, who grew up in Virginia, feels strongly that slavery is not a moral wrong and this basic conflict in his family dogs Brady. Eventually, through a series of events, Brady is forced to confront not only the issue of slavery, but also his own place in the chain of events that connect his family with the Underground Railroad. Set in the 1830's this beautifully written novel tells a touching tale of a boy growing up and trying to find himself. Brady is an engaging character who enjoys being in the woods, raising pet squirrels, being with friends, and simply being a boy. He is also a thoughtful lad who realizes that he sometimes disappoints his father. This conflict of values and beliefs helps create a literary vehicle that also taps into the root cause of the Civil War. Slavery divides Brady's community, his father's church, and his own family. Ultimately, that issue divided Brady's nation and plunged the land into the cauldron of the Civil War. This wonderful novel will interest readers and tell a great story. Originally written in 1960, this recent re-issue by the Trumpet branch of Scholastic is a welcome addition to the field of Civil War related books for younger readers. 2001, Trumpet/Scholastic, Ages 10 & Up, $4.50. ISBN: 0-590-31412-2.

5

Across Five Aprils
Irene Hunt

      There have been many books written about the Civil War but perhaps no novel aimed at younger readers can offer a more touching view of life during that time than *Across Five Aprils*. In this wonderful novel we meet Jethro Creighton and his family. Jethro is nine years old in 1861 when he and his kinfolk first hear about the firing on Fort Sumter. For the Creightons the Civil War comes as a seemingly inevitable curse. Jethro's mother and father watch as the division of the nation plays itself out within their own family. Three of Jethro's brothers, as well as his beloved teacher, all go off to join the Union armies. One brother, through an act of conscience, chooses to head south and become a Confederate volunteer. This act has repercussions for the Creightons as some hardhearted neighbors vent their anger upon the family because of the "traitorous" actions of one of their sons. As the years pass by Jethro remains on the farm watching the seasons change amongst the fields of Southern Illinois. Occasionally letters come home from far away places like Antietam, Fredericksburg, or Chickamauga. Sometimes newspapers reveal details of movements and battles that loved ones are involved in. In one instance a neighbor's son, home due to wounds, shares a tragic reality by describing the death of one of the Creighton lads at an anonymous place known as Shiloh. For another of the Creighton boys the suffering of war becomes too much to bear and he deserts and then hopes to be pardoned through the intercession of a powerful figure in Washington. Eventually, after the passing of five Aprils, the war comes to an end. A Union victory is greeted with joy that is then stifled by the murder of Mr. Lincoln. As loved ones begin to come home a sort of redemption for the Creighton family ensues. The end of the war did not leave this vibrant family untouched. However, it was over and life went on as it did across the American nation. This book contains so many elements of the Civil War that it is amazing. It is a beautifully written book that contains hope and fear, love and anguish, as well as wonderful characters. By reading this novel we come away with a deeper understanding of what the war meant to one Illinois family and what it must have represented to millions of other Americans. 1986, Berkley, Ages 12 & Up, $4.99. ISBN: 0-425-10241-6

6

Pink and Say
Patricia Polacco

      Sheldon Russell Curtis is a teenager serving in an Ohio infantry regiment. He is badly wounded in battle somewhere in Georgia and survives only because of the helping hand of another young Union soldier named Pinkus Aylee. Young Pinkus happens to be black and he and his newfound comrade manage to make their way to the plantation from which Pinkus escaped to join the boys in blue. At the devastated plantation Pinkus finds his mother, Moe Moe Bay, holding fort despite the presence of Confederate "marauders" in the neighborhood. Moe Moe Bay is thrilled to see her baby return home safe and sound and she throws herself into helping Sheldon. While under Moe Moe Bay's care Sheldon comes to see that there were far deeper meanings to the war than he had ever imagined. The two boys become friends and adopt one another's nicknames – hence the book's title, "Pink and Say". Once Sheldon recovers from his wounds the lads determine that it is time to return to their units. Sadly, Confederate irregulars arrive and tragedy besets Pink's family. The boys are then captured and part company at the doorstep to Andersonville Prison. Say is taken off to captivity while Pink meets a different destiny. While Sheldon survives his imprisonment it is at great cost. Based upon a true tale of bravery and comradeship this is a book that will touch your heart. The epic journey of Pink and Say is in many ways an allegory for issues of brotherhood that were fought for and in some ways lost both at the time of the Civil War and in the present. Handed down across four generations, the saga of Pink and Say stands out among Civil War books for children. This simple yet devastatingly compelling story is one that will appeal to and enhance readers both young and old. Accentuated by striking colored illustrations this book is simply a classic. It has also been recently reissued by its publisher in a Spanish edition. 1994, Scholastic, Ages 7 to 10, $16.00. ISBN: 0-590-54210-9

7

Soldier's Heart
Gary Paulsen

In June of 1861 fifteen-year-old Charley Goddard chose to leave his family farm and join the Union Army. He enlisted in the First Minnesota Volunteer Infantry and set off for what he thought would be a short-term adventure. Ultimately, four years later, Charley returned to his home in Winona a drastically changed person. What was to be a brief and adventurous endeavor left a permanent mark upon Charley's life. In his years of service he was to take part in some of the most terrible battles of the Civil War. Starting at First Bull Run the First Minnesota was to become one of the legendary regiments of the Army of the Potomac. On July 2, 1863, during a critical point of the Gettysburg Battle, Charley Goddard and his comrades in the First Minnesota were thrown into the maelstrom of combat to plug a critical gap in the Federal lines. While that engagement proved successful in saving the Union lines it cost over 82% casualties in approximately one half hour. For Charley experiences such as Gettysburg translated into seeing his friends and comrades killed or maimed in combat. Memories such as these wrought a deep and lasting change upon Charley's spirit. When Charley left for war he was a bright eyed and spirited boy. Four years later, Charley Goddard returned to the Northland of Minnesota still a youth at age nineteen. However, he was fundamentally altered by the trauma of war. Charley was a young man with a "soldier's heart"—a description that in later generations would be replaced by "shell shock", "battle fatigue", or "post traumatic stress syndrome". Based upon the real life experiences of Charles Goddard and the First Minnesota this fictional account takes the reader into the swirl and savagery of battle. The millions of farm boys, clerks, mechanics and other civilians who made up the massive Union and Confederate armies came home changed by their exposures. In some instances the patina of old age allowed them to come to grips with what they had seen and done. In other cases, like that of Charley Goddard, life was permanently defined and delimited by the clash of battle. This is a moving novel, written by a masterful craftsman of children's books. It captures the spirit of one person who actually survived the Civil War only to be a very real victim of it. It is good for us to remember the human cost of war and books such as this serve as vivid reminders. 1998, Delacorte Press, Ages 9 & Up, $15.95. ISBN: 0-385-32498-7.

8

When Johnny Went Marching: Young Americans Fight the Civil War
G. Clifton Wisler

Between 1861 and 1865 approximately three million Americans, north and south, joined their respective nation's armies. Among this multitude were tens of thousands of youngsters under the age of eighteen. These young soldiers served in a variety of capacities including musicians, hospital aides, naval powder monkeys, and combat soldiers. The story of these boy soldiers is told in this fascinating book written by one of the leading authors of historical fiction for younger readers. G. Clifton Wisler has written several memorable Civil War novels inclusive of *Red Cap* and *Mr. Lincoln's Drummer Boy*. He also has the honor of having five great-great grandfathers who served in Union regiments during the Civil War. Here, in this outstanding work readers will learn about the travails, accomplishments, and service of a select group of young soldiers. Meet Orion Howe a thirteen-year-old who joined the 55th Illinois along with his brother Lyston and their father. At Vicksburg Orion was part of a hopeless May 1863 assault upon the Confederate lines. When the attack stalled Orion was sent back for much needed ammunition. En route Orion was wounded in his thigh but still suffered through to deliver the request for ammunition. For his efforts Orion Howe was awarded the Congressional Medal of Honor in 1896. On the Confederate side of the line readers of this fine book will encounter James Philip Carver who enlisted in Ector's Brigade of the Army of Tennessee at the age of seventeen. Known as JP and a member of the 32nd Texas dismounted cavalry young Carver was a willing soldier who saw some hard fighting. At Kennesaw Mountain JP suffered a terrible wound through his right lung. Surgeons removed a shattered rib but held out no hope for his recovery. Placed with the hopeless cases JP awoke in the night among a number of dead comrades. With great effort JP dragged himself to the surgeon's tent where he received assistance. James Philip Carver surprised his doctors and survived. He went home, lived through the end of the war, married, fathered thirteen children, and finally died in 1906. The resilience of these two young soldiers wearing blue and gray stands out as a testament to the courage of youth. The history of the boy soldiers of the Civil War is one that will move readers to their core. This book also features a series of wonderful photographs of youthful combatants. Purchase this book and take a few seconds and peer into those faces and then think about children their age and the things they saw and did during the Civil War. 2001, Harper Collins Publishers, Ages 10 & Up, $18.95. ISBN: 0-688-16537-0

9

Lincoln: A Photobiography
Russell Freedman

Winner of the 1988 Newberry Medal as outstanding children's book of that year, this work is simply one of the finest biographies of Abraham Lincoln ever written for young people. Combining an excellent narrative with numerous photos this book provides an in depth, balanced, and moving portrait of the tragic figure that guided the nation through the fiery baptism of the Civil War. Starting with Lincoln's birth in a dirt-poor family and building toward his inevitable meeting with an assassin's bullet, Freedman consistently captures not only Lincoln's story but that of the nation torn asunder as well. Lincoln's life influenced the events of his age and was a direct product of them. In this sumptuous book we come in touch with a leader of great complexity. Lincoln was a man who hated slavery but he was also a person who questioned the ability of the different races to live together. A loving father and husband, Lincoln lived through the pain of losing children and loved ones. Embedded in a very complicated marriage, Lincoln bore the ups and downs of family life against the backdrop of unbelievable responsibility. By presenting Lincoln, his life, and his work in an evenhanded fashion, Freedman allows the reader to appreciate him as a man and not merely a saintly figure of a mythological past. This is a wonderful book and one that will engage and enhance those who read it. 1987, Clarion Books, Ages 10 & Up, $9.95. ISBN: 0-395-51848-2

10

A Separate Battle: Women and the Civil War
Ina Chang

When many people think of the Civil War they conjure up images of battle flags, muskets, soldiers on the march, and the battles that were fought. Yet, at a time when over thirty million Americans lived in the nation only 10% of those citizens actually served in the two armies. Further, fully half the population was naturally made up of women who had very little to do with the actual fighting of battles. In an age when women were viewed as fragile and limited personages, the coming of war created a sudden burst of new experience that changed American society. For mothers seeing their beloved boys go off to an uncertain world in the army staying back home and passively waiting for the results of war was difficult. Faced with this reality, many women chose to work for organizations such as the Sanitary or Christian Commissions. For others, the act of nursing became a means of expressing their patriotism and support of the various causes. On many farms, with men off in the army, the physically numbing work that had to be done fell to women to complete. In a few instances, women actually donned military uniforms and disguised themselves to join in the fighting of the war. Other women left their homes to work in munitions factories. All in all, the lot of women did lead to a 'separate battle' to make a contribution at a time when their nation and families were being torn apart. This 'separate battle' demonstrated that, through the efforts of individuals and the collective millions of northern and southern women, great accomplishments could be wrought. It is these efforts that make up this wonderful study of women during the Civil War. Focusing upon individuals such as Clara Barton, Harriet Tubman, Louisa May Alcott, and Harriet Beecher Stowe as well as the universal work of women this is a beautifully written and amply illustrated history. Those of you who want to know more about an oft times overlooked element of the Civil War would do well to peruse Ms. Chang's masterful book. 1991, Lodestar Books, Ages 10 & Up, $16.00. ISBN: 0-525-67365-2

11

The Boys' War
Jim Murphy

While most Civil War soldiers were men there were many who strode off to join the armies who were in reality children. It would be a rare regiment that did not have at least some boys still in their teenage years hefting a musket and marching along. In other instances lads as young as nine accompanied units in the capacity of drummer boys. Some musicians were very young as were powder monkeys on board the ships at sea. Yet, factors such as minie balls, shot, shells, and disease were no respecters of age. A boy of twelve, living in camp, stood as great a chance of succumbing to illness as any other "soldier". Thus, many of these boys did not survive the war and their childhoods ended in some anonymous hospital bed or a small piece of nameless earth in a farmer's field. The 'boys' war' that Murphy describes is one that split families and plucked young men away from their farms, villages, or towns and set them down into a world they could not imagine. Through tracing the daily life of soldiers, with a particular focus upon the lot of younger boys in uniform, the author provides an insightful and touching historical record. A sharp text combined with many illustrations makes this a valuable teaching tool. Readers will be introduced to the boys and men who fought and died during the Civil War. Their experiences in camp, on the march, in battle, and in hospital are all detailed in this outstanding book. Written with both great skill and great heart *The Boys' War* is a wonderful study in young people trying to find their place in the sun at a time of war. This is a must read book that could well hook a reader's interest in the Civil War. 1990, Clarion Books, Ages 10 & Up, $9.95. ISBN: 0-395-66412-8

Red Cap
G. Clifton Wisler

In 1862, at the age of thirteen, young Ransom J. Powell lies about his age and joins the Union Army as a drummer boy. As a member of the 10th West Virginia Volunteer Infantry Ransom goes off to war expecting to find glory and bright images. What he encounters instead is all the blood and suffering that only warfare can produce. Stricken by these terrible images of death and destruction Ransom then comes to be part of one of the true horror stories of the Civil War. No aspect of that conflict stands out more in terms of pure suffering than the fate of prisoners of war. For no good reason both north and south treated their captive foes in an abysmal manner. For Ransom Powell, and his comrades in the 10th, their fate was to be imprisoned at Andersonville. There, Ransom, still wearing his red musician's cap, struggles to survive in a hellish place. Watching his friends die one by one as starvation and disease run rampant young Ransom comes to question how people can behave as they do. Ransom is also struck by the cruelty of the guards, some of whom are no older than himself. Eventually, Ransom's experiences at Andersonville shape his life in the most basic way. Based upon the actual experiences of Ransom J. Powell, a drummer boy in the 10th who did, indeed, experience prison life at Andersonville, this novel is a striking book. The realities of Civil War life in a prison leap off the pages and challenge readers to look at the issues of cruelty that are inherent in warfare. Through young Ransom J. Powell we come to see what war does to people and how they survive it. 1991, Puffin, Ages 10 & Up, $5.99. ISBN: 0-14-036936-8

13

Numbering All the Bones
Ann Rinaldi

Eulinda is a young girl living on a southern plantation in Georgia. Her brother is away from home fighting during the Civil War. Eulinda worries about her brother, Neddy, and wonders every day if he will return to their home safe and sound. Of course, Eulinda, who is a slave, does not root for the local side in the conflict. As a slave she longs for freedom and prays that the Union army, which Neddy has run away to join, will triumph. The Hamptons, who own Eulinda and her family, happen to live near an infamous Confederate prison camp known as Andersonville. Local residents are fully aware of the terrible suffering that occurs in that hellhole but nothing seems to motivate them to express their concern about the treatment of their fellow human beings who their government holds in captivity. Through a chain of events Eulinda discovers that Neddy is a prisoner at Andersonville. Despite the intervention of Mr. Hampton, who also happens to be Eulinda's biological father, efforts that are made to free Neddy result in failure. Later, when the war ends, Eulinda is called upon to assist a great northern woman, Clara Barton, as she attempts to catalog the many Union men who died at Andersonville. Through these grim efforts Eulinda finds both strength and her future. In *Numbering All the Bones* noted children's author Ann Rinaldi turns her attention to a rather grim topic. Andersonville, and indeed the global treatment of prisoners during the Civil War, was one of the greatest blots upon the American historical record. In this carefully researched novel Ann Rinaldi brings not only the fictional world of Eulinda Hampton to life but also the tragic events that occurred in and around Andersonville.
2002, Scholastic, $4.95, Ages 10 to 14, ISBN: 0-439-46083-2

– Chapter 23 –

"Dear Emma": Letters To & From the Homefront

People of flesh and blood just like any person you may know fought the Civil War. The soldiers who marched off to war proudly wearing their uniforms of blue, gray, or shades of brown left behind loved ones who mourned their absence, feared for their well being and longed for their safety. At home, while the soldiers marched, fought, and died family members carried on the daily tasks involved in everyday life. Women nursed their babies in the absence of the infant's father. Wives girded their loins and took on the previously "manly" tasks of planting crops, managing home finances, and handling business matters. All across the North and the South lives went on—not quite the same—but nevertheless constantly moving ahead despite the drums of war.

In many ways life is basically about relationships. If you stop and think about what matters in life you probably will think about people more than things. Material goods are part of a safe & happy life. It is difficult to imagine happiness in the face of starvation and want. However, it may be even more difficult to imagine true happiness in the absence of caring relationships. The American Civil War—like wars before and after It—shattered literally millions of relationships. No conflict that claimed over 630,000 lives and maimed hundreds of thousands of other men, could possibly avoid these destructive ramifications. Each death or disabling wound claimed not only the recipient but also a web of others who were involved in that soldier's welfare. As the 17th century

English cleric and writer John Donne once wrote, "The death of any man diminishes me, for I am involved in mankind. So, send not to see for whom the bell tolls, for it tolls for thee." The truth of that classic line is borne out when people take the time to look at the human effects that war's grim impact has upon the loving relationships of its participants.

In order to grasp the human cost of the Civil War one can quote statistics and manage data in order to pinpoint the enormity of suffering that accrued from that conflict. Such a macrocosmic approach to empathy development certainly can be a powerful tool. The tremendous number of casualties suffered in the Civil War is ample evidence of the grieving that the American nation withstood during those violent years. Yet, such an approach may be too statistical and sanitized to really understand the way in which every single one of the men killed in the Civil War left a gaping hole in the web of life of all those with whom he once lived, loved, worked, and remained.

Another way of trying to convey the emotional debt that the Civil War exacted is to look at single relationships and how they were fundamentally altered by the experience of war. One such relationship was that developed by two New Jersey residents. In the courting, wooing, and love held between these two common yet unique people, readers may find an even deeper understanding of what war does to people than any facts or figures can convey. These two people are Emma Randolph and Walter G. Dunn and their story is one that remains universal in its lessons.

In 1862 Walter Dunn enlisted in the 11th New Jersey. Like so many of his contemporaries, Dunn did not expect to participate in a war that would ultimately nearly grind his nation into ruin. Dunn marched off with the rest of the 11th with a sense of purpose but also in possession of a secret. Just prior to his departure, Dunn had pledged to maintain an ongoing correspondence with a young woman who had caught his fancy. That young lady, Emma Randolph, was attractive and thoughtful. While Walter and Emma had no clear-cut understanding or engagement they did enjoy one another's company. Hence, a correspondence was struck up and maintained. Every week or so Walter and Emma would sit down, take pen in hand, and scribe out the events of their days. These letters came to be penultimately important to both of them. Indeed, the importance of the letters was so self-evident that they saved most of them. Years later, in a fortuitous turn of events, those letters were unearthed and compiled in a book form. Their content traces both the evolution of a loving relationship as well as the dire cost that war can charge those who cross its path.

    For Walter Dunn active service in the field was short lived but eventful. Dunn had only been in service for a few months when his unit, along with the bulk of the Army of the Potomac, ventured into the Virginia wilderness. Under the audacious but ultimately fumbling command of General Joe Hooker, the Union troops marched into the region near Chancellorsville. There, amidst the roots, branches, scrub, and forest of that wild countryside Walter and his comrades were soundly trounced by General Lee's legions. In the course of the battle Walter was shot through the lungs with the ball deflecting up and finally lodging in his right shoulder.

    Walter was fortunate to survive so dreadful a wound. He lived in an age when medical care was fairly primitive and it is somewhat amazing that he could live through a severe wounding. However, he did and was ultimately evacuated to a military hospital in Baltimore, Maryland. There, during his convalescence, Walter began to write to Emma. Those letters served as a means of communicating with his home and the future that he had some inkling might be so important for him.

    Initially, Walter's letters speak of non-threatening subjects. Often, in these initial letters, Walter mentions the state of his health. For example, in one of his first letters

Walter catalogs the nature of his wound and the treatment prescribed by his attending physician, "My shoulder is nearly well. I have found the ball and am waiting on the Surgeon's motion to have it extracted. He says that it is in a very critical place and that it would not be safe to cut it out now but thinks that in course of time it will work nearer the surface. It is behind the shoulder." (Bailey & Cottom, p., 8)

    Life in the hospital was fairly grim for Walter. In the first few months he often writes Emma about the illnesses that claim some of the residents of his ward. One patient suffers from a spreading infection and must decide whether or not to have his foot amputated. In the end the soldier agreed to the amputation. Walter, who was recovered sufficiently to act as a hospital orderly, assisted in the surgery. He described it in the following manner, "They have taken up two arteries in his foot and tied them to keep him from bleeding to death. I think that if you had seen me when the doctors were performing the operation you would have thought that I was a butcher, I was so covered with blood." (Bailey & Cottom, p. 10)

    On another occasion Walter encountered the spouse of a patient who had recently died. That meeting left an indelible impression upon young Dunn and he shared it with Emma, "A few days ago one of our patients died and about an hour afterward his wife came to see him. I never saw a woman so struck with disappointment as she was when I told her that he had just died. She was out of employment in the city where she lived and the Surgeon in charge gave her employment here as a nurse." (Bailey & Cottom, p. 10)

    As the weeks passed Walter began to describe some emerging feelings he had for the eighteen-year-old Emma. Walter, being just nineteen himself, was relatively inexperienced in amorous affairs and his initial caution in describing any feelings to Emma was quite natural. Yet, by the late fall of 1863 Walter felt he could lift the veil over his emotions a bit. In one letter he hinted at his deepening attitude while also reassuring Emma that their correspondence meant a great deal to him "It is not my desire for any means to cease corresponding with you, the reading of your letters is a source of great pleasure, I only wished to give you to understand that if it was your desire, that I would not be burdensome. Instead of your letters being without interest as you said you supposed they were, they have been the right reverse and I should feel it a great loss to loose (sic) such a correspondence as you have been for over one year." (Bailey & Cottom, p. 18)

This sort of hinting at the feelings he was developing continued for a few more weeks. Then, shortly before Christmas in 1863, Walter became bolder, "Em, we have been corresponding as you will admit for a considerable over a year and now I want you to tell me frankly if you had any other object in view in wishing our correspondence to continue, more than merely a correspondence of friendship." (Bailey & Cottom, p. 22)

Interestingly enough, although Emma's response must have been encouraging as the correspondence continued and deepened, there is no record as to what it exactly was. Walter destroyed Emma's letters in the summer of 1864 when the forces of Jubal Early moved north. While Early's troops were delayed at Monocacy and ultimately stymied near Washington, Walter felt certain that they would head toward Baltimore. He feared that such a turn of events might leave Emma's letters in the hands of invading Confederates. Therefore, Walter chose to burn them rather than risk their forfeiture. While this action may seem somewhat impulsive, and certainly is regrettable from a historian's standpoint, who can truly understand the stress and anxiety that led Walter Dunn to destroy his treasured letters. Nevertheless, following that series of unfortunate events, Walter religiously preserved Emma's letters. That act allows modern readers to see the evolution of one relationship gripped by the passage of armies.

One quality that shines through in these letters is the elemental morality of these two people. Both Walter and Emma were young. Yet, despite their youth, they were willing to bear the burdens of separation and fear that war bred. Likewise, both of these young people were able to see beyond their own selfish needs. At one point Walter was in line for a furlough. This gift of time would allow Walter to return home and see both his family and his sweetheart. Yet, when he knew another soldier's needs, Walter undertook an act of sacrifice that is worth mentioning. In Walter's own words, "I could have had my furlough and been home ere this but I let a young man go in my place who received a letter that his mother was quite sick and as I have had one furlough which he has not, I thought that it would be doing as I would be done by, to let him go first." (Bailey & Cottom, p. 31)

As time passed and Walter and Emma's love and future plans deepened, their separation became more saddening to both of them. One trait that maintained the morale of both of these young people was their deep and abiding religious faith. In the summer of 1864 Walter touched upon this theme of belief in one of his letters, "But we must be content and not complain, for whether in ill or good health we must remember that all comes from the hand of an All Wise Providence and our trials and afflictions here are to show us, our frailty and weakness and fit us, more perfectly, for a happy hereafter. May they not be without effect." (Bailey & Cottom, p.58)

Emma also tried to be stoic in her demeanor. Surely the absence of her beloved fiancée was a burden for her to maintain. Also, while Walter was not in the front lines, he was in constant pain from his wound and exposed to the dreadful miasmas of a military hospital. Yet, Emma often notes "but the longest day will have an end." (Bailey & Cottom, p. 82) But, there were moments in Emma's letters when her sadness is hinted at. In October of

1864 she wrote, "Oh how I miss you Walt. You dont (sic) know.
You cant (sic) half imagine. My feelings compel me to close. I hope your prayers will soon be answered for I'm tired of this, but I endeavor to endure to the end, for I know "tis all for the best"" (Bailey & Cottom 128)

Walter too fell into emotional doldrums at times. He missed seeing and touching his future wife. In response to the sadness felt by Emma Walter wrote, "Dear Emma you said that you missed me very much, you cannot miss me any more than I do you, that is impossible. I have dreamed about you several times since I have returned and oh, such pleasant dreams. I only wish that I might realize them soon. If you were only here tonight I could tell you how much I miss you, not only with words but with my actions as I have a keen desire for a good hug, but that is impossible under the circumstances." (Bailey & Cottom, p. 132)

It is not too difficult to imagine how sad some days were for these two young lovers. In an age when all too many families were receiving notice of sons lost on battlefields, in prison camps, and on sick beds, it certainly was not improbable that Walter might not make it home. Similarly, many of Emma's letters touch upon her own recurring illnesses and the deaths of neighbors at the hands of disease. There were no guarantees that Walter and Emma's long distance courtship would blossom into full flown nuptials. Perhaps such thoughts were darkening Emma's thoughts when she penned the following closing to one of her letters, "My feeling(s) compel me to stop. Oh how I wish you was coming up to see me tonight, but never mind spaces there is between us and how far apart. I think of you always, and remember you as my own Dearest Friend, the one I expect to find "True as the Stars." I have confidence that such you will prove. Good night. Please write soon to your own true and still loving." (Bailey & Cottom, p. 136)

One fear that Emma often refers to is the thought that Walter would succumb to some form of respiratory malady. Emma realized that Walter's grievous wound from the Chancellorsville Battle had damaged his lungs. His visits back to New Jersey when he actually secured a furlough were grand but he was still weakened by his injuries. On several occasions Emma enjoins Walter to try to avoid soldiers ill with breathing disorders. At one point in this correspondence Emma advises Walter as per how to recover from a heavy cold that he reported to her. Emma goes on to caution Walter thusly, "Now I feel as though I ought to caution and give you a little advice, for I am anxious about you. Be verry (sic) careful of your own self Dear Walt, for remember there is a mortgage on you. Will you? Do not expose your self more than is necessary for if you have got such a strong constitution, nothing will help to restore if after once it is gone." (Bailey & Cottom, p. 163)

As is true of all elements of life and existence, time passes and things change. Slowly the war years passed. Events rolled by inclusive of great battles, the surrender of Lee's army, the assassination of President Lincoln, the passing of Union armies along the streets of Washington in the Grand Review, and the disbanding of the mighty hosts that fought the Civil War. Along with these momentous events came smaller but no less important ones. One such happening that surely caused no great media stir was the returning of Private Walter Dunn to his New Market, New Jersey home in July of 1865.

Once home, Walter and Emma wasted very little time in wedding. On September 19, 1865 Walter and Emma were married at New Market's Seventh Day Baptist Church. The young couple, having limited means, moved in with Emma's parents in Plainfield, New Jersey. There, Walter secured work although his profession remains unknown. Sadly, the ravages of war had left a mark on Walter. The weakened lungs that Emma had worried about were to be his downfall. In January of 1866 Walter became quite ill. His disease settled into his lungs and, after a twelve-week illness, Walter died on April 16, 1866. (Bailey & Cottom, p. 248)

  Not long after the death of her twenty-two-year-old husband, Emma gave birth to a daughter. The child was named Mary Emma Dunn but her birth drained Emma. Shortly after Mary Emma's birth Emma became ill and died on August 20, 1866. At Emma's funeral service the presiding minister mentioned that she had gone on to "that eternal world of joy, where now we doubt not, she has been welcomed by her Saviour, and where too she has joined the company of her dear companion, among the blood-washed throng." (Bailey & Cottom, p. 248)

  Less than a single month later the infant Mary Emma Dunn also died. The child's death was recorded in the *Seventh Day Baptist Recorder* with the following commentary, "the last light of the family has expired. Father, mother, and child are now numbered with the dead. They are, we have good reason to hope, an unbroken family in the kingdom of heaven." Whatever one's belief structure may be, it could be justly surmised that, "A war that had already claimed more than six hundred thousand lives, had claimed three more." (Bailey & Cottom, p. 248)

  In the end, the joined lives of Walter and Emma Dunn, as well as their infant daughter, were incredibly brief. Looking back at their letters to and from the homefront readers are touched by the joys and pain that young love can give birth to. Walter and Emma experienced a courtship that possessed all the elements of drama that emerging love can bear. Over time, they came to fall in love. Across a great distance they maintained a jointed love that harbored the possibility of future bliss. However, time and circumstance had other plans for these young folks. They survived the war but not unscathed. The hopes they nurtured across three years of correspondence fell into dust and ashes when confronted by the hard realities of wartime injury and illness in an era when disease was a grim reaper. In Walter and Emma Dunn modern students of the Civil War can get in touch with the human face of that conflict.

The young Dunn's were in no way dissimilar to countless thousands of other people who yearned for a loving life but realized that hopes could be crushed by war. There was a "mortgage" placed upon the happiness of these young people. In a seemingly inscrutable manner the principal and interest on that loan were collected far too soon. But, in recounting the story of Walter Dunn and Emma Randolph Dunn one can virtually touch the human cost of the Civil War, and all wars that are waged. In that way these poignant writings broaden not only one's understanding of the Civil War but also the human condition as well. Yet, readers must remember that this was but one of millions of human interest stories that made up the Civil War. In attempting to recreate those bygone days it is essential to always place a human face upon the history being reenacted. In the letters of Walter & Emma, readers and reenactors alike have several human faces to recall and utilize to inspire a deeper understanding and feeling of compassion for what people of the Civil War era experienced.

Source

Judith A. Bailey & Robert I. Cottom (ed.), *After Chancellorsville: The Civil War Letters*
 Of Private Walter G. Dunn & Emma Randolph, Baltimore, MD: Maryland Historical Society, 1998, 259 pp., $

- Chapter 24 -

"So you want to be a Soldier?"
Tips to Women Portraying Civil War Fighting Men

In the late 1880's when Mary Livermore, a former Civil War nurse and soldier's aid coordinator, heard the speculation that more than four hundred women "bore arms and served in the ranks" of the Union army she recorded in her memoir that although she could not "vouch for the correctness of the estimate," she felt confident that "a larger number of women disguised themselves and enlisted in the service, for one cause or other, than was dreamed of."[1]

While there is no accurate way to actually determine the number of women who donned male attire and went to war as soldiers, scholars of creditable repute have come to some conclusions. Most recently historians Deanne Blanton and Lauren M. Cook, in their comprehensive work *They Fought Like Demons: Women Soldiers in the Civil War*, note, "Approximately three million soldiers served throughout the Civil War. While no one will ever know exactly how many of these soldiers were women, extant documentation suggests they only numbered in the hundreds."[2] Given that tiny number of women soldiers these two capably writers note, "Clearly, the service of these women did not affect the outcome of battles and campaigns, and the service of women did not alter the course of the war. Their individual contributions and exploits are fascinating

---

[1] Tsui, Bonnie. *She Went to the Field: Women Soldiers of the Civil War*. The Globe Pequot Press, 2003, pp. 1
[2] Blanton, Deanne & Cook, Lauren M. *They Fought Like Demons: Women Soldiers of the Civil War*. Vintage Books, 2002, pp. 205-206

but are not the primary reason for their historical significance."[3] The primary significance of these women warriors rests in the fact that, "Women soldiers of the Civil War merit recognition because of the fact that they were there and because they were not supposed to be. They deserve remembrance because their actions made them uncommon and revolutionary, possessed of a valor at odds with Victorian and, in some respects, even modern views of women's proper role."[4]

Given this unusual role for a mid-nineteenth century woman, the image of a Civil war soldier serving while disguising her gender remains a gripping one. As a result, every season, a small percentage of military reenactors is made up of women portraying soldiers. In many cases the women who don military clothing and march or ride out onto the recreated battlefields do a very creditable job of portraying a Civil War soldier. In other instances, the self-evident truth of the living historian's gender and soldierly bearing make that impression at best inaccurate, and at worst discomfiting.

Similarly, every reenacting season a debate occurs as to the value and appropriateness of women serving in the ranks as psuedo-men. For some unit commanders and privates, women who are so committed as to want to recreate a soldier's life are welcome as hearty comrades. Other officers and men sneer at the efforts made by women to recreate a disguised Civil War soldier. For many reenactors the decision as to the validity of a woman's efforts on the reenacting field are driven by the quality of that person's impression and bearing.

Given the fact that every year women do continue or commence military impression in the Civil War reenacting community it is appropriate to highlight some keynote points

---

[3] Blanton & Cook, pp. 206
[4] Blanton & Cook, pp. 206

that might assist in the development & maintenance of impressions that do honor to those intrepid women who fought in the Civil War. What follows are ten areas to consider if you wish to be a soldier while your gender typically would rule that option out. Furthermore, these suggestions may also be of value to officer, NCO's and privates who come into contact with women military reenactors. Each of these topical areas is also accompanied by some historical reference to underscore the fact that women did indeed contribute to the causes for which they fought. In some cases that contribution was minor, while in others it represented not only great sacrifice but also even death.

Maintain a Believable Disguise

In 1911 State Senator Ira Lish backed his automobile out of the driveway of his home in the rural community of Saunemin, Illinois. Unfortunately, Senator Lish struck his hired handyman, Albert Cashier, severely injuring the elderly fellow. During a medical examination of Mr. Cashier the consulting physician discovered that Albert was, indeed, a woman. This fact stuck all who eventually realized the reality of Albert Cashier's gender as remarkable. Not only was Cashier's disguise a contemporary befuddlement but also a historical one as well. For, Albert Cashier, who in reality was Jennie Hodgers an Irish immigrant who came to the United Sates just prior to the Civil War, had proudly served "his" country for nearly four years as a Union soldier in the 95th Illinois.[5]

While Albert Cashier's unmasking has historical interest, it also presents key lessons to modern women intent

---

[5] Romaneck, Erin Elizabeth. *Civil War Stories: Tales of Everyday Soldiers & Civilians.* Unpublished Manuscript, pp. 82-83

upon portraying a Civil War soldier. Albert Cashier was able to maintain her disguise for nearly fifty years. For most of the Civil War Albert Cashier lived, marched, fought, ate, and simply passed time with male soldiers without discovery. In 1914 when, in light of the revelations regarding Albert Cashier's gender, hearings were held to ascertain the validity of "his" ongoing military pension, a number of Albert's former comrades in the 95th Illinois came forward to testify on her behalf. Those veterans' commentaries are enlightening in terms of how successful Albert Cashier was in disguising her true persona.

As part of Albert's defense her counsel asked fellow members of her unit to testify as to her service. None of the veterans questioned in Albert's review hearing had any prior idea that she was a woman. Several of Albert's comrades from the 95th remembered that she had been "shy and hard to know." One Illinois soldier noted that, "Cashier was very quiet in her manner and she was not easy to get acquainted with." Another veteran from the 95th explained how it was possible for Albert to conceal her identity during the war, "When we were examined at induction we were not stripped. We were examined on the same day. All that we showed was our hands and feet. I never did see Cashier go to the toilet nor did I ever see any part of his person exposed by which I could determine the sex. He was a very retiring disposition and did not take part in any of the games. He would sit around and watch but would not take part. He had very small hands and feet."[6]

Every veteran who testified at Cashier's hearing was surprised to discover that she was a woman. When asked to identify Albert from pictures of her as a soldier and as a male civilian, Robert D. Hannah of the 95th expressed his surprise, "About two weeks ago I learned that Albert D.J. Cashier is a

---

[6] Wiley, Bell. *The Life of Billy Yank: The Common Soldier of the Union.* LSU Press, pp. 338.

woman. I never suspected anything of that kind. I knew that Cashier was the shortest person in the Co. I think he did not have to shave. There has never been any doubt in my mind since it came out that Cashier was a woman but that it is so. I have not seen Cashier since a few years after the war. I am not able to identify the right hand figure in the double picture you show me. It has been too long ago, and fifty years make too many changes in a person for me to identify the right hand figure. I have no doubt about the left hand figure being the picture of Albert D.J. Cashier."[7]

In terms of modern day applications of these historical facts, it is essential that any woman who wishes to maintain an authentic impression of a soldier must develop a believable material interpretation. Such a reenactor's uniform must disguise their gender in an effective way. Hairstyles should be adopted that conceal the reality of said person's gender. Make-up and any other vestiges of femininity are not permissible. In all regards, a woman soldier must look like a man and be able to pass muster as such both with other reenactors and the general public while maintaining a low profile.

Proficiency in Drill

"When you think of me think where I am. It would make your hair stand out to be where I have been. How would you like to be in the front rank and have the rear rank load and fire their guns over your shoulder? I have been there my Self."[8] In this way Lyons Wakeman of the 153rd New York described one aspect of his training as an infantryman. In reality, Lyons Wakeman was Sarah Rosetta Wakeman, a young woman who had chosen to enlist in the

---

[7] Military & Pension Records of Albert Cashier, National Archives, pp. 5
[8] Burgess, Lauren Cook (Ed.). *An Uncommon Soldier: The Civil War Letters of Sarah Rosetta Wakeman, 153rd Regiment, New York Volunteers, 1862-1864,* Oxford University Press, 1994, pp.26-27

Union army after previously working as a canal boatman in the pre-war years. In this comment, and throughout Private Wakeman's letters home to her family, a theme is revealed—being a soldier meant mastering the drill.

Throughout her letters Sarah Rosetta Wakeman revealed a trait that was common among many of the recorded women soldiers of the Civil War. For Sarah, and her female compatriots, it was essential to master drill in order to maintain the believability of their disguise. A poorly drilled soldier drew attention from officers and others. Such attention could easily lead to scrutiny, discovery, and ultimate banishment from the unit. Therefore, women soldiers had to become proficient in the machinations and facings inherent in Civil War drill.

Drill was an innate reality in the lives of Civil War soldiers. As Lyons Wakeman noted in a letter written in October 1863, "We are adrilling (sic). Company drill in the morning and a battalion drill in the afternoon. For my part I like to drill. I think a Skirmish drill is the prettiest drill that ever was drill. I have got so that I can drill just as well as any man there is in my regiment. When Colonel Davis gives a order I know what the regiment is agoing (sic) to do just as well as he does."[9] In another entry Wakeman simply states, "I like drill first rate."[10]

For contemporaneous female living historians who either are or anticipate carrying out a male soldier impression, these words must be taken to heart. Drill is a basic fact-of-life for reenactors as it was for actual Civil War soldiers. Being adept at drill demonstrates a commitment to both the hobby of reenacting and the historical research that should be part of it. A woman soldier who is a laggard in drill will draw negative attention to her, be obvious to spectators, and pay no real homage to the women of the

---

[9] Burgess, pp. 48
[10] Burgess, pp. 25

1860's who she is recreating. Know the drill and become proficient in it or lay down your musket, cavalry sword, or artilleryman's garb.

Demonstrate Sturdiness & Toughness

Civil War soldiers lived rough-and-ready lives. They slept outdoors in all sorts of weather. On the march they slogged through mud, waded streams, ate dust, and endured blistering heat. Food was often non-existent or abominable. Medical care was intermittent and often of low quality. All in all, the life of a Civil War soldier in the field was tough and required a sturdy disposition.

Among the women who undertook the role of a Civil War soldier in the actual conflict many of them demonstrated a level of toughness that was striking. Elvira Ibecker, alias Charles Fuller of the 46th Pennsylvania, was noted for "his" ability to both drink whiskey and chew tobacco. Confederate Melverina Peppercorn also chewed tobacco and later recalled being able to spit its juice more than ten feet. Loretta Velasquez, who adopted a Confederate officer identity, learned to smoke cigars while in military service. Martha Parks Lindley of the 6th U.S. Cavalry learned to smoke a clay pipe while serving as a soldier.[11]

In regards to toughness Lyons Wakeman comes to the forefront as an example of how at least one woman withstood the bullying that sometimes occurred in units. In January 1864 another member of her company, who was a noted troublemaker and bully, prodded Wakeman into a scrap. Latter Sarah Rosetta Wakeman described the outcome of that fight in one of her letters home, "Stephen Wiley

---

[11] Blanton & Cook, pp. 53

pitched on me and I give him three or four good cracks and he put downstairs with him Self."[12]

Another way in which women soldiers demonstrated their toughness was in terms of language. No woman wishing to be accepted as a man could be shocked by the rough soldier's language that was heard in camp and on the field. Any sort of prissy or sissified attitude would quickly draw suspicion and unwanted attention. Therefore, some women soldiers became quite adept at bandying about the profanities that are part and parcel of being a soldier. One woman soldier, Ella Reno, was jailed for two weeks as punishment for cursing out a superior officer. Three Confederate women who were discovered to be female while imprisoned at Cairo, Illinois were described as "reckless and profane with their profane and vulgar comrades." In another instance a guard at the Carroll Prison in Washington, D.C. described two female inmates in this way, "They are a tough couple and talk worse than any degraded witch possibly could. They are impudent and can beat any private in the oath uttering line."[13]

Reenactors who adopt a male impression need to be able to fit in with the guys. They must be capable of shouldering the burdens of the job. Likewise, they cannot be outwardly uncomfortable when men discuss things that are profane or lascivious. The life of a soldier was hard and hardening. Therefore, it is essential for a female military reenactor to emulate women such as Confederate Melverina Peppercorn who could shoot as well as the twin brother she enlisted with and was "as strong as a man." A woman in the modern reenacting ranks must adopt an attitude similar to Albert Cashier who one comrade described as able to "do as much work as anyone in the company." And finally, a female reenactor wishing to do justice to the women of the

---

[12] Cook, pp.60-61
[13] Blanton & Cook, pp. 53

past should learn from the example of an unnamed woman who enlisted in the 1st Kentucky Infantry (US) and was described by a contemporary journalist in this manner, "She performed camp duties with great fortitude, and never fell out of the ranks during the severest marches."[14]

Develop a Soldierly Bearing

In 1882 at a pension hearing on behalf of Sarah Edmonds who served in the war under the alias Frank Thompson, one of her comrades-in-arms from the 2nd Michigan Volunteer Infantry said the following, "More than one member of the company can attest…Frank's manly bearing, soldierly qualities, kindness, and devotion to the sick deserve to be recognized in a liberal and substantial manner."[15]

This ability to become a good comrade while demonstrating a soldierly bearing was essential for women who hid their gender identity while serving in the Union and Confederate military forces. Similarly, women who wish to carry off a successful male impression in the reenacting community must also be able to demonstrate such soldierly bearing.

At the time of her enlistment in the Confederate army Loretta Velasquez was determined to be "as good a man as any of them."[16] In a similar vein Sarah Wakeman reported her first winter camp experiences in this way, "The weather is cold and the ground is froze hard, but I sleep as warm in the tents as I would in a good bed."[17] In a post-war article a reporter described former Union soldier Martha Lindley as "a good soldier…and never shirked any of the unpleasant

---

[14] Blanton & Cook, pp. 53
[15] Tsui, pp. 7
[16] Tsui, pp. 29
[17] Burgess, pp. 21

duties of the men at the front."[18] Lindley herself modestly described her efforts as a Union cavalryman, "I did the best I could in the service of my country...Although I am only a woman, I think I can say without egotism that there were worse soldiers than I in the service."[19] Confederate Jane Perkins was much more bold than Lindley when, in June of 1864 after her capture, she defiantly told a Union provost marshal at Point Lookout Prison that she "could straddle a horse, jump a fence and kill a Yankee as well as any rebel."[20]

    This type of mental toughness and commitment to the role of being a soldier is essential to being a successful male impersonator in the reenacting ranks. In order to carry that sort of impression off a woman must have both mental and physical conditioning that meets the demands of the job at hand. Women soldiers of the Civil War were committed to their personal and national causes. They were often stoic even in the face of death. One need only recall the image of Sarah Wakeman who was felled by chronic diarrhea during the ill-fated Red River Campaign of 1864. Alone in a hospital bed in New Orleans, Sarah Wakeman slowly withered away. At no point did she reveal her female identity. In the end she died and was buried in New Orleans without military or hospital staff realizing that he was a she.[21] It was this type of bravery and commitment that allowed Lyons Wakeman to exist as a military recruit. It remains the sort of commitment to the role of a soldier that is required of modern day reenactors wishing to emulate their historic female predecessors.

Perform Realistically in Combat

---

[18] Blanton & Cook, pp. 75
[19] Blanton & Cook, pp. 75-76
[20] Blanton & Cook, pp.76
[21] Funkhouser, Darlene. *Women of the Civil War: Soldiers, Spies, and Nurses.* Quixote Press, 2004, pp.54

In August 1863 Sarah Rosetta Wakeman wrote to her parents about the possibility of impending combat, "I don't know how long before i shall have to go into the field of battle. For my part i don't care. I don't believe there are any Rebel's bullet made for me yet. Nor i don't care if there is. I am as independent as a hog on ice. If it is God will for me to fall on the field of battle, it is my will to go and never return home."[22]

This spirit was not uncommon among Civil War soldiers in general, and those female ones in particular. Looking back at the performance of Albert Cashier one of her sergeants in the 95th Illinois said, "He might be the littlest Yankee in the Company, but by golly, he darn sure carries his share of the fight!"[23]

At Cold Harbor in 1864 the Union Army of the Potomac suffered one of it bloodiest repulses. Yet, the Federals did manage to capture a few Confederate prisoners in that engagement. Among these Rebel captives was one artillery NCO who turned out to be a woman. This female cannoneer was described by one of her captors in this fashion, "We did capture a full-fledged artillery woman who was working regular at the piece, she was very independent and saucy as most Southern ladies are."[24]

Women soldiers were in battles and became casualties. In some cases women soldiers paid the highest price a soldier can be asked to contribute—death. In a letter home a member of the 1st Minnesota Artillery wrote home to his sister and recounted the following anecdote, "One of the members of the 1st Kansas Reg't died in the Hospital…After death the somewhat startling discovery was made by those who were preparing the body for burial, that their companion beside whom they had marched and fought for nearly two

---

[22] Burgess, pp. 42
[23] Dawson, Lon. *A.K.A. Albert D.J. Cashier.* Illinois Veterans Home, 1999, pp. 11
[24] Blanton & Cook, pp 22

years was a woman. You can imagine their astonishment. The Reg't is camped near us and I went to the Hospital and saw her. She was of pretty good size for a woman with rather masculine features. She must have been very shrewd to have kept her secret so long when she was surrounded by several hundred men."[25]

In terms of reenacting applications of the fortitude shown by the original women soldiers of the Civil War, there are several lessons to be learned. In reenactment battles women in the ranks must be as well drilled and versed in regards to maneuvers, safety, and weapon handling, as is the norm for their unit. Women military reenactors must have a fitness level adequate to allow them to cope with the rigors of weather, effort, & the elements that are a part of the reenacting world. Finally, in combat reenactments, women living historians must portray wounds, death, flight, and steadfastness in the way in which their historical predecessors would have. Dangers exist in many aspects of reenacting. Nowhere is it greater than when combat is simulated. Women wishing to participate in that psuedo-combat experience must have the skills and attitudes necessary to both maintain a realistic persona and behave in a safe & responsible manner on the field of battle.

Understand the Historic Motivations Involved

In many ways a woman wishing to become a military reenactor shares some of the same motivations her historic predecessors held. Among these were and are patriotism, a search for comradeship, an independent spirit, and a yearning for adventure.

In 1861 Sarah Edmonds felt a powerful inner drive to volunteer and serve in the Union army. In later years she described her feelings at that pivotal time in her life, "The

---

[25] Blanton & Cook, pp. 99-100

great question to be decided…what can I do? What part am I to act in this great drama?"[26] Sarah Edmonds decided to don male clothing and join the army in pursuit of what she described as "an entirely new kind of life."[27] Edmonds also was not content "to stay home and weep" while her male counterparts sacrificed everything for a cause she believed in.[28]

    Once in service many women soldiers developed deep and abiding friendships with their comrades. In camp, on the march, and while in combat women soldiers bonded with the men with whom they shared the dangers and vicissitudes of military life. In her experience Sarah Edmonds lived to see one of her closest friends slain in battle. Afterwards Sarah Edmonds described her feelings, "There was a strong bond of sympathy existing between us, for we both believed that duty called us there, and were willing to lay down even life itself, if need be, in this glorious cause. Now he was gone, and I was left alone with a deeper sorrow in my heart than I had ever known before."[29] Friendships such as the one shared by Sarah Edmonds and another member of her regiment would have been virtually impossible in civilian society. Therefore, this type of comradeship often became a defining part of a woman soldier's experiences in the war.

    In the 1860's, as now, there were women who chose to join the army out of a deeply felt sense of patriotism. Yes, in the Civil War, as in contemporary reenacting, there were women who initially volunteered because they thought the experience might be adventurous, glorious, or fun. After that initial naïve belief was drowned by the realities of actual war or the hardships of wearing Civil War reproduction uniforms

---

[26] Tsui, pp 10
[27] Garrison, Webb. *Amazing Women of the Civil War*. Rutledge Hill Press, 1999, pp. 13
[28] Tsui, pp. 11
[29] Tsui, pp. 19

on hot summer days, other motivations were necessary to maintain a woman in the ranks. None was or is more powerful than belief in a cause.

While she was serving, Sarah Edmonds described why she chose to fight and remain in service, "Perhaps a spirit of adventure was important, but *patriotism* was the grand secret of my success."[30] Thus, a woman may well be motivated to reenact as a Civil War soldier as an act of homage to beliefs held in the 1860's or as an embodiment of love felt for her modern homeland.

An independent spirit was another reason why women volunteered to fight in the Civil War. One need only read the following section of one of Sarah Rosetta Wakeman's letters to see that she possessed an indomitable and quite independent will, "I don't want you to mourn me for I can take care of my Self and know my business as well as other folks know them for me. I will Dress as I am a mind to for all anyone else (cares), and if they don't let me Alone they will be sorry for it."[31] At a later date Sarah Wakeman described herself as "tough as a bear."[32] There is little doubt that Lyons Wakeman was well served by his actual female personality hidden beneath the folds of her sack like uniform.

Looking back it is easy for a woman wishing to pull off a solid Civil War soldier impression to find diverse motives for the real-life female soldiers who fought and died in that divisive conflict. Therefore, both as a valuable element of historical knowledge, and as a reflective element of an individual's impression, it is necessary for women who choose this uncommon impression, to understand the multi-faceted social & economic reasons why women actually did join up and fight in the Civil War.

---

[30] Tsui, pp. 20
[31] Burgess, pp. 31
[32] Burgess, pp. 58

Concluding Thoughts

In a variety of ways women soldiers in the Civil War stand out despite their relatively insignificant incidence. In an age when women were considered virtual property it was striking to find a small band of them so powerfully motivated that they adopted the role of a combat soldier. In fact, when several women were discovered in the ranks, they were considered insane and were treated as such.[33]

Yet, despite the relatively small number of documented female Civil War soldiers, their contribution at a time when women's liberation was more than a century away, stands out as revolutionary and exceptional. As Blanton & Cook note in their pivotal study of women soldiers, "By simply changing a set of clothes, changing a name, changing a hairstyle, and adopting a male alias, many women found that they could easily bypass all of society's barriers to creating a decent, comfortable, and independent lifestyle for themselves."[34]

Given the powerful stories that have been uncovered by journalists and historians regarding the small cadre of women soldiers whose identities were ultimately uncovered during or after the Civil War, there is little doubt that the draw of such a reenacting impression can be very powerful indeed. However, if a woman is intent upon developing and burnishing such a military impression it is incumbent upon her to research and study the lives and methods of actual female Civil War soldiers. Therein lie the core values and basic premises around which to craft a valid woman soldier impression. It is out of the lives of real world Civil War women who took up arms and served their respective causes that their contemporary heirs in the reenacting community should search for guidance. Once these sources of

---

[33] Romaneck, pp. 83
[34] Blanton & Cook, pp. 39

information have been mined, then comes the time to select an authentic and discrete uniform, learn the drill, perform well on the field of battle, be a good comrade, act in a soldierly manner, understand your motives, and serve with honor. These were the traits shared by the women who fought in the Civil War. These too should be the qualities that mark the impression of a woman wishing to pay respect to those brave females who stepped forward in such an uncommon way.

- Chapter 25 -

A Soldierly Bearing: Maintaining A Soldierly Bearing

"Dear Wife—Kiss the baby for me and Write as soon as you get this…when I write again I suppose I shall tell you if I am spared how being on a battle feels." (McDonald 5) In this way Private John Paddington of the 24th Michigan closed a letter home to his wife on the eve of what was to be one of the most violent elements of his life. Within a very few hours of writing this letter, Private Paddington, and the other soldiers of the Iron Brigade of which he was but one member, were to fight at South Mountain and then again near the Dunker Church at Antietam. The following summer, on July 1, John Paddington would die at Gettysburg. But, despite his mortality, one thing that Private Paddington shared with so many other Americans of his age was the experience of combat during the Civil War.

In our own age when living historians strive to recreate the lives of men such as John Paddington it would, perhaps, be a valuable lesson to look back at some of the features of soldier's lives that were common for the wartime era. In gleaning what can be learned from a few such elements of daily life amongst Civil War soldiers reenactors can improve their impressions, enhance their experience at events, and draw themselves into a deeper and potentially more meaningful impression. What follows are a handful of suggestions aimed at enhancing the experiences available to reenactors when they enter the field at events. These suggestions are drawn from the words of Civil War soldiers and relate to a few themes that may be relevant at many living histories, small-scale events, regional encampments, and even large-scale national reenactments.

A Narrow Deadly Space

At Champion's Hill Samuel H. M. Byers of the 5th Iowa saw combat up close and personal. Byers spent much of the battle heavily engaged with the Confederates but, afterwards, he had to admit to a fact commonly encountered by many combat veterans, "The Rebels in front we could not see at all. We simply blazed at their lines by guess, and occasionally the blaze of their guns showed exactly where they stood." (Hess 10)
Similarly, Rice C. Bull of the 123rd New York who saw combat at Peach Tree Creek near Atlanta fought what appeared to be a deadly but invisible enemy, "During the afternoon the enemy made five charges on our line, coming at times within one hundred feet, yet I did not see a single Johnnie. The clouds of smoke from the muskets of both sides…poured down on us to hide everything but the flash of the enemy's guns that gave us their position." (Bull 149)

The experiences of these two Civil War veterans are instructive as to what reenactors can and should expect at events. If there are enough fighting men to make an event noteworthy there will be smoke, confusion, and concentration that will limit a person's focus to a very narrow space. Participants at national events will find that once the scenario begins their attention will and should be narrowed to the immediate area around them and to their front. Just like the Civil War soldiers who fought in battles involving tens of thousands of men, so too, the reenactor will find that their perception of a fight will shrink down to the tunnel line of their vision. That narrow and deadly space represented the final aspect of many real life Civil War soldier's existences. For a reenactor, rather than bewailing the limitations of the experience, perhaps grasping it will better prepare a participant for a more authentic encounter.

Sing Out Your Joy

Looking back on an experience during the 1862 Peninsula Campaign in Virginia a Confederate major wrote, "I shall never forget the first time I heard "Rally Round the Flag." Twas a nasty night during the "Seven Days Fight," and…it was raining. I was on picket when, just before taps, some fellow on the other side struck up that song and others joined in the chorus until it seemed to me the whole Yankee army was singing…I am not naturally superstitious, but I tell you that song sounded to me like the "knell of doom," and my heart went down into my boots; and though I've tried to do my duty, it has been an uphill fight with me ever since that night." (Silber 8-9)

One element of Civil War soldier's existence that still rings true as a stirring fact of life in reenactment camps is music. Think back to times you have sat around a campfire singing songs, listening to a harmonica, or catching the fading notes of a distant fife and drum corps. Music is auditory emotion that releases a wellspring of thoughts, feelings,
and actions from its audience. Therefore, if you would like to better appreciate your reenacting experience take some time and learn a few songs. Do not feel shy about joining in on the march, in camp, at church services, or at the campfire. Do not worry about your personal musicality. Simply sing out in joy or sorrow as our predecessors did during the actual Civil War.

The Touch of Elbows

"The man who can go out alone and fight against overwhelming odds is very rare, and for every one such there are thousands who can "touch the elbow" and go forward to what seems almost certain death." (Hess 110) In this way E. L. Marsh, and Iowa volunteer, described an almost universal truth of Civil War fighting. Soldiers who, on their own, might have fled from the inherent dangers of battle, stood firm or advanced because they were part of a trusted group.

    For Civil War soldiers the initial draw of volunteering may have varied from a search for adventure to true patriotism but after "seeing the elephant" most men fully realized just how deadly fighting was. Once those men were "veteranized" by the clash of arms it was much more difficult to block out the realities of what combat actually represented. But, nonetheless, the men did a creditable job and the war was waged. Perhaps the following words of John W. DeForest of the 12th Connecticut offer some clue as to why this occurred, "The fragment of my old company, in its last fight with a gallant enemy, made charge after charge under a corporal. "You don't go into such a hole because you like it," explained a trooper, describing a dash through a canon-swept valley, "you go in because you are ashamed to go back on the boys." (Hess 110)

    In terms of modern day applications, what reenactors can grasp is the sense of comradeship that is created in a unit. Once you have experienced events, marching, camp life, and the seemingly countless hours of travel that are required to get to some events a bonding occurs among people. On hot days you look out not only for yourself but also for your comrades. In poor weather you expect a helping hand to find a dry place just as you would offer one to a fellow unit member. In battle, an emphasis on safety and comfort for everyone around you becomes a shared responsibility. In drill, the effectiveness of everyone becomes a matter of each individual's performance. In the end, the "touch of elbows" represents the communion that Civil War veterans depended upon and which reenactors should strive to internalize and embrace.

Calmness in the Storm

Looking back on his first combat experience and Iowa soldier recalled, "The first shot I fired seemed to take all my fear away and gave me courage enough to calmly load my musket and fire it forty times." Likewise, Edgar Emberly of the 61st Illinois also reported a similar calm that descended upon him after the fighting started, "I did not feel anything strange on first going into battle; we were drawn up in line of battle (and) I was looking for the secesh as ever I did for a squirrel." (Hess 127) Conversely, Rice Bull remembered a much grimmer mindset before battle, "Looking down the line of our Company as the yelling of the enemy came nearer and nearer to us, I judged that everyone felt about as I did; there was no levity now, the usual joking had ceased and a great quiet prevailed. I could see pallor on every face as we brought hammer to full cock. I believe every arm trembled as we raised our guns to our shoulders to fire but all eyes were to the front, not one looked back." (Bull 55-56)

Regardless of which side men fought on, their combat experiences represented an equal opportunity for death or wounding. On reenactment fields there are lessons to be learned from the attitudes of these, and oh so many other, Civil War veterans. If you are a relative novice entering into your first few battlefield reenactments, pay close attention to the drill, fire cautiously, aim above targets, and control the nerves that are rising up in you. If you are a veteran do the same things but also keep an eye out for your less experienced comrades. In all cases, refrain from horseplay or slapstick actions when you come onto the field. Yes, there were grim humored moments just before battles but they were not the norm. Maintain a soldierly bearing that bespeaks your calmness, caution, and fatalism in the face of the coming storm. Act like a soldier and you will provide a better experience for yourself and everyone around you.

See the Beauty that Surrounds You

In my own reenacting career I have been fortunate enough to see sights that stay with me in their beauty. The fall colors in the Shenandoah Valley at Cedar Creek stand out in my mind's eye. The morning mist rising ethereally above a small Confederate cemetery near Resaca remains looked in my memory banks. Watching the Confederate advance at the largest recreation of Pickett's Charge in reenacting history still gives me pause. In reenacting, and the places it brings a living historian to lies the possibility of great beauty, emotion, and commemoration. Yet, these elements are also a direct connection with the lives of veterans who fought in the actual war.

Even in combat situations, some Civil War veterans were still able to catch a glimpse of the beauty that surrounded them. Frederick M. Woodruff was a Union soldier in the 2nd Missouri Cavalry. In April 1864 Woodruff was under the command of Frederick Steele and was on a raid in southern Arkansas. Just before an engagement with Confederate cavalry Woodruff's regiment paused in a field full of wildflowers. On the horizon Woodruff could see the Rebels forming in line of battle. In the foreground the field was a blaze of early spring color as the flowers were blooming. A hummingbird, oblivious to the coming battle, flitted near Woodruff as it fed on some of the brightly colored flowers. Years later, when he wrote about his wartime experiences, Woodruff could still recall that image, "I contrasted strongly in my mind the peace of this near picture, the picture of the flitting bird, with the angry scene to our front." (Hess 132)

If a soldier of the verge of battle could take the time to appreciate the wonders of nature, how difficult can it be for a reenactor who does not experience the dangers of a Civil War soldier to follow suit? When you are in the field take note of the world around you. Look at the whitetail deer that is scared out of camp when you first set up. Take in the mountains and ridges in the distance and wonder at their nature. Get up early and watch the mist rise above camp. Look at the frost on the ground and take in the utter complexity of its structure. Live life rather than simply totaling up just another event.

Know When You are Played Out

Wilbur Fisk was a sturdy soldier in the 2nd Vermont. As a veteran in one of the better regiments in the Army of the Potomac, Fisk was by all standards a tough and enduring soldier. However, even so staunch a fighting man as Wilbur Fisk had limitations. At the Wilderness in May of 1864 Fisk found himself separated from his unit. In the confusion of that forest battle Fisk joined a group of stragglers and determined that he had seen enough fighting for one day, " I had been fighting to the best of my ability for Uncle Sam's Constitution, and now I thought it of about as much importance to me individually, to pay a little attention to my own." Fisk had seen enough and even though he felt some slight twinges of conscience he was determined to find a safe place to recover so that he could fight again another day, "I should have been ashamed of such conduct at any other time, but just then all I thought of was a cup of coffee, and a dinner of hard tack. The regiment might have been ordered into another battle, and every man of them been killed, and I shouldn't have been ashamed that I wasn't with them, My patriotism was well nigh used up, and so was I, till I had some refreshments." (Fisk 216-217)

If so toughened a veteran as Wilbur Fisk knew his limitations, so too should modern day reenactors. Conditions during a reenactment can be very challenging.

Bodies not conditioned by years of hard work on the farms or in the factories of the 19th century may wilt under the hard hand of marching, heat, or pack load. The ages of many reenactors are more than double the average age of Civil War recruits. Therefore, it is wise to know your limitations and not push beyond them. If you are tired—sit down. When it is hot—find shade. Drink enough water to hydrate. Play only when you have the strength to do so. Do not ignore injuries or hurts. Use your brain as well as your heart and you will go farther in the hobby.

Understand the Causes

Writing home to his family Henry N. Blake of the 11th Massachusetts bluntly described his views as to why he was fighting, "The religious belief of the army was simple, and consisted of two articles of faith; first, that "a man will die when his time comes"; and secondly, that "a soldier who is slain in the service of his country is sure to enter the gates of heaven." The arguments of books and the sermons of divines could not undermine these ideas, in the sincere profession of which thousands fought and died upon the battle-field." (Hess 94-95)

Civil War soldiers, North & South, fought for individual reasons. However, in most cases a combination of loyalty, a sense of personal duty, patriotism, fatalism, or other understandable emotions under girded their service. For men to have endured what Civil Wars soldiers were compelled to, required a high degree of motivation. In order to pay homage to those bygone veterans and their families it is necessary for a living historian to look within themselves and discern why they reenact. Is it because of the joy of comradeship? Do you go into the field because of the adrenaline rush of being in a mock battle? Is your hobby a form of commemoration for an era that for some reason grabs you? Regardless of the reason(s) it is important to at least be aware of what factors motivate you to wear wool and do what you do. Out of such awareness comes a deeper appreciation of and connection to the motivations of the men who actually fought the war. They too had to search within themselves and find reasons to persevere. Should less be expected of us now?

Sources

Bull, Rice C. *Soldiering: The Civil War Diary of Rice C. Bull, 123rd New York Volunteer*
    Infantry. San Rafael, CA: 1977.

Fisk, Wilbur. *Hard Marching Every Day: The Civil War Letters of Private Wilbur Fisk,*
    1861-1865. Lawrence, KS: The University of Kansas Press, 1992

Hess, Earl J. *The Union Soldier In Battle: Enduring the Ordeal of Combat.* Lawrence,
    KS; The University of Kansas Press, 1997.

McDonald, Archie P. *Primary Source Accounts of the Civil War.* Berkeley Heights, NJ:
    Enslow Publishers, Inc., 2006

Silber, Irwin. *Songs of the Civil War.* New York, NY: Columbia University Press, 1960

The Faded Stone

The marker rested in an old part of the cemetery.
Rain and time had worn away much of the lettering.
The passing of days & years left it tilted and sunken.
The passerby stopped and looked down.
Here rested a soldier of days gone by.
Was he a kind and decent man?
Did he have a wife and child?
How was his body brought to this final resting place?
Beneath the sod his humble remains still rest.
Whatever earthly sins or worthy deeds are long over.
He wore the coat of blue as so many others did.
On some far off field he fell.
Killed by a brother clad in gray or butternut.
Now, all that remains is the slanting and faded stone.
Each life gone by has a history.
Rascals & cowards—saints and stalwarts—they all served in turn.
The faded stones and weathered monuments are more than bric-a-brac.
Each stone represents a life once lived—hopes & dreams—fears & courage.
In pausing at the old stone we look both backwards and forwards.
Each of us is mortal—we will have our final moment.

Pay heed to the sacrifice of those who went before.
In those old stones and faded memories resides our
connection to the past.
This single soldier's marker symbolizes the time he
lived and our mortality.
Take heed—remember—then walk away to ponder
our comings and goings.
Those who served in those long gone days have had
their
day—what will our legacy be?

(Evergreen Cemetery—DeKalb, Illinois)

Homage To the Men of '61

The fifer's notes fly over the green field.
Drums mark time for the men.
A steady wind carries the black powder smoke away.
Colors catch the breeze and stand at attention.
The long gone war is resurrected on an Illinois plain.
Moving lines of men in blue & gray recreate the dance of death.
In the ranks each soldier sees their tiny field of vision.
No sweeping perspectives for these men.
They see the world of war through a narrow tunnel framed by their own experience.
Cannons fire and shake the earth.
Men fall in imitation death and wounding.
The woolen uniforms soak with sweat even on a mild fall day.
In the end, the dead arise to accept the crowd's accolades.
The reenacting ends—all is well.
Years ago such scenes maintained their lethality.
Those broken bodies did not ruse again to dust off and straighten themselves.
But, those days are gone & by all too many forgotten.
All that remains of those fallen soldiers are their memories.

Through recreating such men's fate we pay homage to them.
In these actions lies a key to their suffering resting unforgotten.
This is the charge and the task at hand.
It is a worthy one offered up with respect.

(Dollinger Farm Civil War Days, Minooka, Illinois)

ABOUT THE AUTHOR

GREG M. ROMANECK has been interested in the Civil War since childhood. Since 1992, Greg has participated as a reenactor in both infantry and artillery organizations. It was through those first hand experiences that much of the information contained within *A Civil War Reenactor's Guidebook* came into play. In addition, Greg has published well over 100 articles on Civil War themes in publications such as *America's Civil War, Camp Chase Gazette, The Artilleryman, The Civil War News, Citizens' Companion & Civil War Historian*. Greg has also published several booklets and three books dealing with Civil War history. Over the years the primary focus of Greg's Civil War research has been social history and more specifically the lives of everyday soldiers and civilians. Greg also writes extensively on other subjects inclusive of psychology, education, backpacking, leadership, and poetry. Greg lives in DeKalb, Illinois along with his wife, Jane, and their three children. In the world of work Greg is the Director of Human Resources for the Batavia Public School District #101 in Batavia, Illinois.

www.ingramcontent.com/pod-product-compliance
Lightning Source LLC
Chambersburg PA
CBHW070730160426
43192CB00009B/1379